Cambridge Elements ≡

Elements in Philosophy of Law
edited by
George Pavlakos
University of Glasgow
Gerald J. Postema
University of North Carolina at Chapel Hill
Kenneth M. Ehrenberg
University of Surrey

CONTENT-INDEPENDENCE IN LAW

Possibility and Potential

Julie Dickson
University of Oxford

CAMBRIDGE
UNIVERSITY PRESS

Shaftesbury Road, Cambridge CB2 8EA, United Kingdom

One Liberty Plaza, 20th Floor, New York, NY 10006, USA

477 Williamstown Road, Port Melbourne, VIC 3207, Australia

314–321, 3rd Floor, Plot 3, Splendor Forum, Jasola District Centre,
New Delhi – 110025, India

103 Penang Road, #05–06/07, Visioncrest Commercial, Singapore 238467

Cambridge University Press is part of Cambridge University Press & Assessment,
a department of the University of Cambridge.

We share the University's mission to contribute to society through the pursuit of
education, learning and research at the highest international levels of excellence.

www.cambridge.org
Information on this title: www.cambridge.org/9781009468091

DOI: 10.1017/9781009000673

First published 2024

A catalogue record for this publication is available from the British Library.

ISBN 978-1-009-46809-1 Hardback
ISBN 978-1-009-00975-1 Paperback
ISSN 2631-5815 (online)
ISSN 2631-5807 (print)

Content-Independence in Law

Possibility and Potential

Elements in Philosophy of Law

DOI: 10.1017/9781009000673
First published online: December 2024

Julie Dickson
University of Oxford

Author for correspondence: Julie Dickson, Julie.dickson@law.ox.ac.uk

Abstract: This Element examines the notion of content-independence and its relevance for understanding various aspects of the character of law. Its task should be understood expansively as encompassing both enquiry into that which makes law into what it is and enquiry into what law ought to be, which values it ought to serve, and which aspects of its character may play a facilitative role in law realising aspects of its potential. Many existing discussions of content-independence focus largely on the justificatory aspects of content-independence: whether and, if so, how there can be content-independent reasons for action or content-independent justifications of rules, and the extent to which political obligation is content-independent. This Element, too, examines such issues but also seeks to explore an additional possibility: that the notion of content-independence can illuminate issues regarding law's existence, identification, and systematicity.

Keywords: content-independence, jurisprudence, philosophy of law, identification of law, legal system

ISBNs: 9781009468091 (HB), 9781009009751 (PB), 9781009000673 (OC)
ISSNs: 2631-5815 (online), 2631-5807 (print)

Contents

1 Introduction

This Element is animated by an inkling long harboured by its author: that the notion of content-independence can illuminate a range of phenomena relevant to understanding the character of law. The choice of words here is significant, and it is important to emphasise from the outset that some key terms should be understood in an expansive and ecumenical manner. In referring to 'the notion of content-independence' I begin to indicate (1) that in this work 'content-independence' is to be understood broadly and as encompassing a wider range of phenomena than is customary in the works of some legal and political philosophers, and (2) that in my understanding of it and of some debates in which it features, content-independence seems more of a notion, or a cluster of several related ideas, than a sharply defined unitary object of inquiry. In making this point I do not intend to denigrate the work of other legal philosophers on content-independence in law. Indeed, amongst the works of both advocates and sceptics of content-independence can be found high-quality discussions infused with much philosophical erudition and technical prowess (see, e.g., Adams 2017; Green 1988; Markwick 2000, 2003; Raz 1986, 2001; Sciaraffa 2009; Valentini 2018).

This work does not attempt to rival such discussions, although surveying and commenting on aspects of some of them, and on some of the themes that they raise, features in various of its chapters. Notwithstanding the existence and quality of such works, there seems to me to be an explanatory remainder which can fruitfully be explored by 'zooming out' from some of the details of the relevant debates and considering the possibility of, role for, and potential of, content-independence in law in a broad manner and across various contexts in understanding different facets of law.

As regards the claim that the notion of content-independence can illuminate important aspects of 'the character of law': this term should also be understood expansively as encompassing both (1) enquiry into that which makes law into what it is and (2) enquiry into what law ought to be, which values it ought to serve, and which aspects of its character may play a facilitative role in realising aspects of its potential.

What follows, then, is an exploratory journey around what content-independence in law is, what roles it plays and has the potential to play, and how it connects with other aspects of law's character. My approach takes as its cue the aims of the Cambridge Elements in Philosophy of Law series: to review the state of the art in the field and attempt to bring better into focus fresh research agendas for the future. I also attempt – although I accept that I may not fully succeed and that the extent to which it is possible to succeed may vary from issue to issue and from section to section in this work – to avoid, where possible and to the extent possible, 'taking sides' as regards the correctness of various general theories of the nature of law. For one thing, it is impossible in an Element such as this to vindicate the truth and explanatory adequacy of any general theory of the nature of law. For another, my inkling that the notion of content-independence can illuminate important aspects of the character of law includes the thought that some aspects of content-independence have an important role to play in *any* account of law's character and potential.

The Element is structured as follows. Section 2 – Characterising Content-Independence – considers various ways of thinking about the character of content-independence that can be found in the relevant literature in legal and political philosophy. This discussion sets out some possibilities for the discussions to come, and begins to consider which aspects of, and accounts of, the notion of content-independence are apt for understanding different facets of law's character. Section 3 of the Element – Content-Independence in Law: Existence and Identification – engages with the role that content-independence plays in understanding various issues regarding how law is created, identified, and applied. Many existing discussions of content-independence focus largely on what we might call the justificatory aspects of content-independence – for example, whether and, if so, how there can be content-independent reasons for action (Adams 2017; Green 1988; Raz 1986) or content-independent justifications of rules (Gur 2011; Raz 2001), and the extent to which political obligation is content-independent (Klosko 2011, 2023; Valentini 2018; Walton 2014; Zhu 2018). I want to suggest and explore an additional possibility: that the notion of content-independence can also help us to understand aspects of law's existence conditions and its identification conditions. Section 4 – Content-Independence in Law: Aspects of Justification – explores some of the justificatory aspects of content-independence in law. In particular, it considers the role of content-independence in understanding the authority of law, the character of legal rules and their impact on our practical reasoning and our governance structures, and whether and, if so, how it could be justified to act as law requires.

Sections 3 and 4 of this Element are each subdivided into two. The first subsection of each explores issues surrounding the character and possibility of content-independence in law with respect to the issues addressed in that section. The second subsection then takes us forward to consider the potential of content-independence in law with respect to those, and related, issues. The subsections on the potential of content-independence in law engage with what content-independence in law may be good for, and what role it can play in law's ability to facilitate the attainment of certain values. They hence explore various senses in which content-independence in law contributes to law's ability to be as it ought to be, and to realise those values that it should. Fruitful directions for fresh research agendas are highlighted throughout the Element and are drawn together in summary form in Section 5, the concluding section. This Element does not attempt to offer a conclusive account of all aspects of content-independence in law. Rather, the hope is that it will illuminate a variety of questions and puzzles for future research as regards our understanding of this notion, the range of contexts in which it operates, and the values that it can help to realise.[1]

2 Characterising Content-Independence

This section considers some ways of thinking about the character of content-independence that are found in the relevant literature in legal and political philosophy. As mentioned in Section 1, many existing discussions of content-independence focus largely on what we might call the justificatory aspects of content-independence: for example, whether and, if so, how there can be content-independent reasons for action (Adams 2017; Green 1988; Markwick 2000, 2003; Raz 1986) or content-independent justifications of rules (Gur 2011; Raz 2001), and the extent to which political obligation is content-independent (Klosko 2011, 2023; Valentini 2018; Walton 2014; Zhu 2018). I suspect that this focus influences which aspects of the notion of content-independence feature most prominently in the relevant literature. A shift in focus may be needed as regards those aspects of content-independence we emphasise, so that this notion can illuminate a broader range of questions regarding law, such as questions surrounding its creation, identification, and application. This should become clearer as the discussions in this section, and the one that follows it, proceed.

2.1 Content-Independence: Three Characterisations

As several theorists writing about content-independence note, it can appear to be a somewhat nebulous concept (Adams 2017; Gur 2011; Marmor 1995: 345; Valentini 2018: 136). In considering some of the relevant literature, it seems helpful to set out three possible characterisations of it that I will refer to as:

(i) the independent of content characterisation
(ii) the intentions as reasons characterisation
(iii) the container characterisation.

---

[1] A short work such as this Element is inevitably limited in the range of literature that it can consider in exploring the topic at hand, and I am acutely aware that the literature in question is largely (though not exclusively) drawn from the Anglo-American tradition in legal and political philosophy. My hope, however, is that the works highlighted (see also Dagger and Lefkowitz 2021; Green 2023) and the issues for further discussion raised can assist the interested reader in traversing other avenues of thought for themselves.

It should be noted that these characterisations may be neither mutually exclusive nor jointly exhaustive. Indeed, as the discussion unfolds it will become clear that some legal philosophers' accounts of content-independence combine aspects of them. This being so, the three characterisations should be viewed as indicating different areas of emphasis as regards how content-independence is to be understood that are each useful in exploring that notion, and in focussing on which aspects of it are relevant to understanding various features of law.

2.1.1 The Independent of Content Characterisation

Several theorists characterise content-independence in a manner reflective of its name. Legal philosopher H. L. A. Hart is sometimes credited with having coined the term in an early article (Hart 1958) and with developing it in 'Commands and Authoritative Legal Reasons', in his *Essays on Bentham* (Hart 1982). In this latter work, Hart characterises content-independence in the context of understanding commands, and the manner in which they are supposed to impinge on our practical reasoning processes, as follows:

> Content-independence of commands lies in the fact that a commander may issue many different commands to the same or to different people and the actions commanded may have nothing in common, yet in the case of all of them the commander intends his expressions of intention to be taken as a reason for doing them. It is therefore intended to function as a reason independently of the nature or character of the actions to be done. In this of course it differs strikingly from the standard paradigmatic cases of reasons for action where between the reason and the action there is a connection of content: there the reason may be some valued or desired consequence to which the action is a means, (my reason for shutting the window was to keep out the cold) . . .. (Hart 1982: 254–255)

This passage reveals that, in fact, Hart's characterisation of content-independence in the context of commands involves a combination of two of the characterisations identified above: (i) the independent of content characterisation and (ii) the intentions as reasons characterisation. The intentions as reasons characterisation will be addressed in Section 2.1.2; our current focus is on the independent of content characterisation.

The first point to note is that Hart is focussing in this passage on content-independent *reasons for action* in the form of commands (and, as his discussion proceeds, in the form of what he terms authoritative legal reasons). He characterises such reasons for action partly by way of contrast and in terms of what they are not. The contrast is with what Hart says are 'standard paradigmatic cases of reasons for action where between the reason and the action there is a connection of content' (Hart 1982: 254–255): for example, I prepare carefully for my teaching for the reason that so doing will help my students to grasp complex material vital for their studies, or I take a certain medication for the reason that it helps me to manage a medical condition and so remain in good health, which is a valuable aim. In such cases, the reason and the action for which it is a reason seem connected in a direct way, and it is obvious from the face of the situation that the reason warrants my performing that action. Hart's contention is that, by contrast, in the case of a content-independent reason for action, the connection between the reason and the action for which it is a reason is dislocated, such that the reason – for example, that one has been commanded to do so – is supposed to function as a reason in some manner that is on the face of it unconnected to the content of the action required – for example, to take a certain medication. The dislocation can be further emphasised by pointing out, as Hart does, that, in the case of content-independent reasons, the reason is supposed to be able to function as a reason for a range of different actions with different, and indeed perhaps even contradictory, contents. That one has been commanded to do so is intended to function as a reason whether the content of the action required by the command is that one should take a certain medication, refrain from taking a certain medication, or administer a certain medication to another person.

Three points seem to emerge from Hart's 'independent of content' characterisation:

(1) Content-independent reasons for action are non-standard or non-paradigmatic cases of reasons for action.
(2) They are non-standard or non-paradigmatic in that the usual connection between a reason and the action for which it is a reason is dislocated.
(3) One marker of a content-independent reason is that it is intended to, and is supposed to be able to, function as a reason to do a range of actions with different, indeed perhaps even contradictory, contents.

These points are also prominent in Joseph Raz's characterisation of content-independent reasons:

> A reason is content-independent if there is no direct connection between the reason and the action for which it is a reason. The reason is in the apparently 'extraneous' fact that someone in authority has said so, and within certain limits his saying so would be reason for any number of actions, including (in typical cases) for contradictory ones. A certain authority may command me to leave the room or to stay in it. Either way, its command will be a reason. This marks authoritative reasons as content-independent. By this feature they can be distinguished from many reasons, including various other kinds of utterances that are reasons. (Raz 1986: 35)

These points also find their place in Raz's characterisation of the manner in which rules function as reasons for action:

> It [the justification of why a rule is binding] is content-independent in that it does not bear primarily on the desirability of the acts for which the rule is a reason. Here we see clearly how rules differ from other reasons. The insightfulness and subtlety of a novel are reasons for reading it because they show why reading it is good. But the considerations which show why the rule [of a club where members cannot bring more than three guests to social functions] is binding, i.e. why it is a reason for not bringing more than three guests, do not show that it is good not to bring more than three guests. They show that it is good to have power given to a committee, and therefore good to abide by decisions of that committee. But that can justify a variety of rules. (Raz 2001: 8–9)

An intriguing suggestion mentioned briefly in both Hart's and Raz's character-isations of content-independence is that it can be *a matter of degree* or, perhaps, depending on the context, that certain phenomena may be both content-independent and context-sensitive (see Hart 1982: 255; Raz 1998: 274–275 and 2001: 8–9). This suggestion is examined further in Sections 3 and 4 of this Element.

Other theorists, too, understand content-independence in a manner tightly connected to its name, and hence espouse variants of what I have termed 'the independent of content characterisation' (see, e.g., Duff 1998; Green 1988: 40–62; Shapiro 2002: 389–90). However, this view also has its sceptics. Stefan Sciaraffa, for example, in his aptly titled 'On Content-Independent Reasons: It's Not in the Name' argues that the independent of content characterisation, although widespread, is significantly misleading as it focusses on the wrong feature of content-independent reasons in attempting to delineate them as dis-tinctive (Sciaraffa 2009). He contends that our understanding of the character, grounds, and limits of content-independent reasons for action will be improved if we move to a characterisation of them that emphasises as their distinguishing feature 'that content-independent reasons are intentions' (Sciaraffa 2009: 234). Paul Markwick also casts doubt on various interpretations of the independent of content characterisation, particularly in respect of the point mentioned earlier that one marker of a content-independent reason is that it is intended to, and is supposed to be able to, function as a reason to do a range of actions with different, indeed even contradictory, contents (Markwick 2000).

2.1.2 The Intentions as Reasons Characterisation

As noted already, some theorists contend that the distinguishing feature of content-independent reasons is that intentions are supposed to function as reasons in their case. Sciaraffa argues that 'an agent has a content-independent reason to φ if and only if someone's intent that she φ is a reason for her to φ' (Sciaraffa 2009: 234), such as when, in a military context, a commanding officer intends a subordinate to obey her command for the reason that the commanding officer has issued it and intends that the command be obeyed because it is her command. Sciaraffa parses this as follows:

> (1) the speaker intends to get the hearer to act in a certain way; (2) the speaker intends for the hearer to recognize that the speaker intends for the hearer to act in that way, and; (3) the speaker intends for the hearer's recognition of the speaker's intent in (1) to function as the hearer's reason for acting as the speaker intends. (Sciaraffa 2009: 246)

As a result of his doubts that the independent of content characterisation outlined in Section 2.1.1 offers either a coherent or a helpful account of content-independent reasons, Sciaraffa advocates that the intentions as reasons characterisation be adopted to the *exclusion* of the former (Sciaraffa 2009). He hence appears to view these two characterisations on an 'either/or' basis and opts decisively for the intentions as reasons view.

Other theorists, however, appear to regard the independent of content characterisation and the intentions as reasons characterisation not as rivals but as complementary, with each emphasising different aspects of, and bringing out different facets of the puzzles regarding, the notion of content-independence. This can be seen from Hart's account of content-independent reasons for action, which, as noted in Section 2.1.1, features aspects of both the independent of content characterisation and the intentions as reasons characterisation: 'Content-independence of commands lies in the fact that a commander may issue many different commands to the same or to different people and the actions commanded may have nothing in common, *yet in the case of all of them the commander intends his expressions of intention to be taken as a reason for doing them*' (Hart 1982: 254, emphasis added). Raz, too, augments his independent of content characterisation of content-independent reasons with the intentions as reasons point: 'A reason is content-independent if there is no direct connection between the reason and the action for which it is a reason. *The reason is in the apparently "extraneous" fact that someone in authority has said so*' (Raz 1986: 35, emphasis added). Moreover, in later work focussing specifically on the content-independence of rules, and the way in which rules function as reasons for action, Raz notes and makes use of this second facet of content-independent reasons to highlight a puzzle it engenders: how can it be that people can create reasons just by acting with the intention to do so? (See Raz 2001: 6.)

As noted in Section 2.1.1, Hart and Raz both draw attention to the fact that content-independent reasons for action appear to be non-standard or non-paradigmatic cases of reasons for action. One facet of this already mentioned is that the usual connection between the reason and the action for which it is a reason (for example: I take a certain medication for the reason that it helps me to manage a medical condition and so remain in good health, which is a valuable aim) is dislocated or displaced. As the point emphasised by Raz just now indicates, another facet of the 'non-standard' character of such reasons is that what *is* supposed to supply the reason instead is somewhat opaque and, on the face of it, does not obviously amount to a reason for action at all. If, while walking beside the River Thames in Oxford, I meet a colleague who says to me, 'Hi, Julie! You are required to jump in the river now because I say so, and because I intend my saying so to function as a reason for action for you', then I do not regard this as creating for me a reason for action, and I hope I would not be alone in this assessment.

Augmenting the independent of content characterisation of content-independent reasons with the intentions as reasons characterisation hence illuminates and brings better into focus the puzzles to which such reasons give rise. An interesting variation on the view that content-independent reasons are to be understood in terms of both the independent of content characterisation *and* the intentions as reasons characterisation can be found in a helpful discussion of whether legal rules are content-independent reasons offered by Noam Gur (2011). Gur draws a distinction between what he terms a strong sense of content-independence and a weak sense of content-independence. He contends that the former – the strong sense – is constituted by the reason for action being independent of the content of the action required *and* the reason for action stemming instead from the fact that law requires the action, whereas the latter – the weak sense – involves only that the reason for action is independent of the content of the action (Gur 2011: 178–183). In drawing this distinction, and in his ensuing discussion of whether legal rules are content-independent reasons for action in either the weak sense or the strong sense, Gur raises another important point in considering the intentions as reasons characterisation of content-independence. To put the matter in the terms that Raz does, already mentioned (Raz 2001: 6), in asking how it can be that people can create reasons just by acting with the intention to do so, are we asking whether such intentions *on their own* can create reasons for action, or whether they create reasons for action only when combined with certain other factors, for example when there are valid moral reasons establishing that law has legitimate authority? On the latter understanding, law generates content-independent reasons for action because it says so *and* because the fact of it saying so is crucial in some way to it being able to fulfil the conditions of being a legitimate authority and hence serve some value(s) in human affairs. This issue is discussed further in Section 4 in considering whether the notion of content-independence can play a justificatory role as regards aspects of law's function and manner of operation as it is claimed to do in, for example, Joseph Raz's normal justification thesis of authority (see, e.g., Raz 1986: chapters 2–4 and 1994a).

As with the independent of content characterisation, the intentions as reasons characterisation has its doubters. Gur may count as one of these, at least on a certain interpretation of the question of whether legal rules can be content-independent reasons for action in Gur's strong sense of content-independence (Gur 2011: 184–196, 209–210). On a variation on the theme mentioned at the close of Section 2.1.1, Paul Markwick also doubts that legal reasons can be content-independent, at least on a certain interpretation of the intentions as reasons characterisation of content-independence (Markwick 2003). When taken together with his argument doubting the existence of content-independent reasons as understood in various interpretations of the independent of content characterisation (Markwick 2000), Markwick offers us a meticulously argued and thought-provoking stance as regards the very possibility of there being content-independent legal reasons at all. He does, however, leave open the possibility of there being such reasons on what he regards as a less problematic interpretation of their character (Markwick 2003: 61; for in-depth discussion of Markwick's views in this regard, see Flanigan 2020: 164–173).

2.1.3 The Container Characterisation

In an article considering various issues regarding and challenges to the notion of content-independence, Nate Adams introduces a helpful idea (albeit one that could benefit from further consideration in future research): that a content-independent reason has 'a container as a constituent part and changing the content of that container does not determine whether the agent has a reason and does not determine the weight of that reason' (Adams 2017: 149). In common with several of those characterisations of content-independence considered in Sections 2.1.1 and 2.1.2, Adams' account emphasises that there is something non-standard or non-paradigmatic about content-independent reasons. Drawing a contrast with 'the way reasons normally work' (Adams 2017: 144), he contends that '[t]he most distinctive and important characteristic of content-independent reasons is the way they sever the normal connection between the merits and demerits of acting in some way and whether one has a reason to act in that way' (Adams 2017: 145). Thus far, Adams' account sounds similar to the independent of content characterisation discussed in

Section 2.1.1. However, when he turns to the issue of what *does* supply the reason for action in the absence of the usual connection between a reason and the merits or demerits of the action, Adams makes two interesting additional points: (1) that some reasons for action that are content-independent can be said to be *source-dependent* (Adams 2017: 147); and (2) that considerations such as source-dependence, and other factors relating not to reasons' content, should be understood as *containers*, and that, in one form or another, all content-independent reasons have containers as one constituent part of them (Adams 2017: 147).

Adams illustrates these ideas via a familiar example: that of a parent exercising authority over their child by requiring them to go to bed and, when asked for reasons why by the child, replying not in terms of the benefits of a good night's sleep but by invoking the fact that the child's parent has said so (Adams 2017: 145). Adams imagines two alternatives to this first scenario: one in which the parent still issues the directive but changes its content to 'Eat your peas' (Adams 2017: 146), and another in which the directive remains 'Go to bed' but is issued not by the parent exercising parental authority but by a stranger (Adams 2017: 147). According to Adams' analysis, in the second alternative scenario the action required remains the same, but the existence and the weight of the reason for action change because the source has changed: 'If we change the source of the speech act, as in the stranger case, the existence and the weight change but the favored action does not. The source of the command is wrong, so the child has no reason (of no weight) to go to bed' (Adams 2017: 149). By contrast, in the first scenario, though the required action changes, because the source (the parent, exercising parental authority) does not change, and as the source functions (in Adams' terminology) as a container which can have varying content, the existence and the weight of the reason for action for the child do not change. Adams summarises his container characterisation as follows: 'In sum: a reason is content-independent *iff* it has a container as a constituent part and changing the content of that container does not determine whether the agent has a reason and does not determine the weight of that reason. The existence and weight of a content-independent reason instead depend on features of the container' (Adams 2017: 149).

Adams believes that his container account can successfully parry the challenges to accounts of content-independence mounted by Markwick (2000, 2003) and Sciaraffa (2009) referred to earlier in this section. He further contends that, as in the parental authority example, the paradigmatic case of a content-independent reason is a reason constituted by a speech act (Adams 2017: 149–150), but also notes that some theorists, for example Marmor and Raz, employ the content-independence/content-dependent distinction in contexts beyond speech acts (Adams 2017: 157–158, referring to Marmor 1995: 346 and to Raz 1999: 48 and 51). Adams' container account provides an expansive and flexible manner of characterising the notion of content-independence. This being so, it can be useful in broadening the notion of content-independence so that it can play a useful role in our understanding of law beyond questions concerning its ability to provide authoritative content-independent reasons for action.

2.2 Content-Independence in Law: Which Characterisation?

Which characterisation of the notion of content-independence should we adopt in order better to understand aspects of law's character? It is tempting to ask whether we have to choose at all: one possibility mentioned at the outset of Section 2 is that the three characterisations may not be mutually exclusive and should be understood rather as indicating different areas of emphasis as regards how content-independence is to be understood. In general, I am sympathetic to the tenor of this approach. My instinct, however, explored further in the discussions to come, is that which of these characterisations proves to be most apt and illuminating also varies according to the aspect(s) of law's character and operation under consideration.

For example: Section 3 of this Element considers the role of content-independence in better illuminating aspects of law's existence and identification. It examines whether the notion of content-independence can shed light on various questions and puzzles regarding how law is created, identified, and applied by human-made social institutions and those who act on such institutions' behalf. As previously noted, many existing discussions of content-independence lean heavily towards taking content-independent *reasons for action* as their primary explanandum. Section 3, however, engages with issues that can be viewed as relatively distinct from, and in a sense are prior to, questions concerning law's ability to generate reasons for action and whether those subject to it ought to obey it. Whether or not legal directives – in general, of a particular jurisdiction or on particular matters within a jurisdiction – provide reasons for action and generate obligations to obey them, such directives *exist*, are created, identified, interpreted, and applied, and have an important impact on the lives of those they affect as a result. My instinct – explored in Section 3 – is that matters highlighted by characterisation (i) – the independent of content characterisation – and by characterisation (iii) – the container characterisation – are particularly apposite in illuminating matters concerning law's creation, identification, and application. These characterisations have features which enable them to operate across different contexts, and so to be put to good explanatory use beyond their customary context of explaining content-independent reasons for action.

Section 4 of this Element engages with various aspects of law's justification conditions, such as whether and, if so, when, why, and how law has legitimate authority over us such that its directives give us reasons for action. In my view, characterisation (ii) – the intentions as reasons characterisation – is particularly illuminating in this context. Although aspects of characterisations (i) and (iii) are also relevant here, the intentions as reasons characterisation has particular explanatory power as regards bringing out certain puzzles regarding whether and, if so, how the fact that law requires something can function as a reason for action of those subject to it, including in some situations where law is morally mistaken about what there is reason to do.

Across both Sections 3 and 4, individual points highlighted by certain theorists in the previous discussion of the three characterisations also prove especially apposite for understanding both the possibility and the potential of content-independence in legal governance contexts. Raz's point that content-independence may, in a certain sense, be a matter of degree and various theorists' point that there is something non-standard, or non-paradigmatic, about content-independent reasons for action are both important in this regard and can illuminate and aid our understanding of certain familiar yet puzzling features of law's operation.

These points are intended only to convey a flavour of the discussions to come regarding (i) law's existence and identification and (ii) aspects of law's justification. It is to the first of those discussions that we must now turn.

3 Content-Independence in Law: Existence and Identification

As outlined in Section 2.2, the explanatory power of the three characterisations of content-independence offered in Section 2.1 may vary according to which facets of law are under consideration. The focus in this section is on the existence and identification of law. My working hypothesis is that factors highlighted by characterisation (i) – the independent of content characterisation – and by characterisation (iii) – the container characterisation – are particularly apposite in illuminating issues concerning law's creation, identification, and application. A further aim of the discussion in this section is to highlight a fresh research agenda for the future regarding the notion of content-independence in law. Legal philosophers should explore further the idea of content-independence not only as regards the existence and character of content-independent reasons for action but in terms of how it can aid aspects of our understanding of law's existence as a social, institutional, and systemic phenomenon. It should be noted that, in making this point, I am not claiming that one group of puzzles about law is more important, more central, or more worthy of study than another. My own view is that legal philosophy is a 'broad church' (Dickson 2015), that we should encourage and welcome a variety of forms of exploration of a variety of issues, topics, and puzzles in legal philosophy, and that such pluralism in enquiry is one of the hallmarks of a flourishing discipline (Dickson 2022: chapter 4).

3.1 Possibility

Those living in law-governed societies are aware that the actions of institutions play a significant role in creating, identifying, and applying the law. We know that institutions such as parliaments, courts, passport offices, and the police exist, and that the actions and processes of those institutions, and of those who act on their behalf, are important in making law, implementing law, and resolving disputes that occur involving law. Such awareness is widespread and need not be implausibly complex in character. One does not have to be involved with law in a professional capacity to know that its institutions, the processes occurring in those institutions, and the actions of its officials are woven through many aspects of our lives in society. Those who *are* involved with law in a professional capacity of course have a more focussed and acute understanding of the institutions and processes upon which law's operation rests.

Theories of law also exhibit a strong interest in such matters. One focus is the issue of how the law is to be identified, and the role of legal and political institutions and their processes in identifying it. In some general theories of law – that is, theories of law's character wherever it is found, and not merely in this or that particular legal system – such issues emerge in the form of questions concerning the criteria of legal validity. Legal positivism, for example, is associated with the view that the criteria of legal validity in any jurisdiction must conform to what is sometimes called 'the social thesis': that the existence and the content of the law are ultimately to be determined by reference to social facts – in particular, by reference to law's social sources – and not by reference to the merits of the legal norms in question.[2] To give a simplified example from

---

[2] I begin with legal positivism because, in my view, it furnishes useful examples of how exploration of the notion of content-independence may aid our understanding of certain issues relating to the existence and identification of law. As I noted in Section 1 of this Element, I am attempting – although I accept that I may not fully succeed – to avoid, where possible, 'taking sides' as regards the correctness of various general theories of law. Moreover, in my view, some aspects of the notion of content-independence have an important role to play in *any* successful account of law's character and potential. Other approaches to understanding law, including some contemporary natural law approaches, and Ronald Dworkin's interpretivist approach are considered later in this section.

the United Kingdom context: that a bill has been passed by majority votes in the House of Commons and the House of Lords and has received the Royal Assent – that it has those institutional processes and interactions as its source and that directives emerging from that source are recognised by UK legal officials as constituting valid law – is what makes it into part of the statutory law of the UK. A bill which those institutional processes have rendered an Act of Parliament is valid law even if it lacks merit to the point where it should never have been introduced to or supported in Parliament in the first place, or recognised or enforced by anyone, and a bill which is meritorious but which failed to receive the required votes in Parliament is not valid law.

Although several legal philosophers have called into question the usefulness of grouping together views about law's character under the banner of 'legal positivism', including some of those to whom the term might be thought to apply (Gardner 2001: 278; MacCormick 2007: 278; Raz 2007: 35), some version of the view outlined earlier regarding criteria of legal validity and the identification of law is espoused by numerous legal philosophers (Coleman 2001; Gardner 2001, 2007; Green 2008; Green and Adams 2019; Hart 2012; Kramer 1999, 2004; Marmor 2001, 2006; Raz 2007, 2009a; Shapiro 2000, 2009; Waluchow 1994). I mention that these theorists espouse *some version of* the view outlined earlier partly to take account of the fact that there is a split within legal positivism concerning the stringency of the thesis that the existence and the content of the law are to be determined by social facts and not by reference to law's merits. For those in the so-called 'exclusive positivist' or 'hard positivist' camp – including Raz, Marmor, Gardner, and Shapiro – law is to be identified solely by reference to its social sources, whereas for so-called 'soft positivists' or 'inclusive positivists' – including Hart (at least in the posthumously published 'Postscript' to *The Concept of Law*: Hart 2012: 244–237), Waluchow, and Kramer – the merits of a legal norm may contribute to determining its legal validity and content, but only if, in a given legal system, source-based considerations render those merits relevant to such determinations. So, for example, for soft or inclusive legal positivists, if a norm in a constitution (itself recognised as valid law according to that system's criteria of legal validity) requires that no statute shall be legally valid unless it is consistent with fairness and equality, then the (moral) values of fairness and equality are thereby included in, or incorporated into, the test for legal validity in that jurisdiction, and the identification of its law will be partly dependent on its conformity with merit-based considerations. Exclusive legal positivists deny that merit-based considerations indicated or referred to by social sources thereby become incorporated into the law. As a result, they offer different explanations of legal phenomena such as equality or fairness clauses in constitutions (for one such attempted explanation, see Raz 2004; more generally, for discussion of exclusive versus inclusive legal positivism, see Giudice 2008; Green and Adams 2019; Himma 2005; Kramer 2004; Marmor 2001; Raz 1994a; Shapiro 2000, 2009, 2011; Waluchow 1994).

To return to our main topic: can the notion of content-independence help to illuminate issues and puzzles regarding the existence and identification of law such as feature in the accounts of law outlined earlier? I believe that it can, especially if we focus in this context on some of the matters highlighted by characterisation (i) – the independent of content characterisation – and by characterisation (iii) – the container characterisation of content-independence.[3]

Let us start with the latter. The discussion in Section 2.1.3 noted that Adams' container characterisation includes the following two points:

(1) some reasons for action that are content-independent can be said to be *source-dependent* (Adams 2017: 147);
(2) considerations such as source-dependence, and other factors relating not to reasons' content, should be understood as *containers*, and, in one form or another, all content-independent reasons have containers as one constituent part of them (Adams 2017: 147).

Adams developed his container characterisation in the context of seeking to understand content-independent reasons for action. In my view, however, the points that his characterisation highlights can fruitfully be transposed to the context of law's creation and identification. Consider the example given earlier: that of the criteria of legal validity according to which bills are turned into statute law in the UK's Westminster Parliament. That parliamentary process functions as one source-dependent 'container' in respect of how law is created, and how it is to be identified as legally valid, in the UK. The 'container' of the process of passing through majority votes in the House of Commons, the House of Lords, and receiving the Royal Assent is the vehicle by which law is created from proposals, debates, and bills. Statutes emerging from that container and/ or, in some cases, from slightly modified versions of it[4] are identified and applied as law by courts, the police, and other legal officials in virtue of having that container as their source. Moreover, the content of what emerges from the container of that UK parliamentary process can vary considerably without such variations affecting whether it counts as part of the law. Indeed, successive governments with very different ideas and policy stances make law using the

---

[3] See Section 2.1 for discussion of each of these characterisations.
[4] For example, according to the terms of the Parliament Act 1911 (www.legislation.gov.uk/ukpga/Geo5/1-2/13/contents) and the Parliament Act 1949 (www.legislation.gov.uk/ukpga/Geo6/12-13-14/103/contents).

UK parliamentary process with vastly differing content, and a later government may repeal an Act of Parliament passed by an earlier one and enact a replacement with contrary content.

This last point – that the same parliamentary process can create statutes with a vast range of different, in some circumstances contradictory, content – also chimes well, albeit in a slightly different key, with facets of the independent of content characterisation of content-independence. In Section 2.1.1 it was noted that an aspect of this characterisation is that one marker of a content-independent reason for action is that it is intended to, and is supposed to be able to, function as a reason to do a range of actions with different, indeed perhaps even contradictory, contents (Hart 1982: 254–255; Raz 1986: 35). Transposed to the context of law's creation and identification, this point can be rendered as: one marker of content-independent law-creation and law-identification processes is that they are intended to be able to create legal norms with a range of different, and in some circumstances contradictory, contents.

All this being so, the parliamentary legislative processes outlined in the example can fruitfully be understood as being – to a significant extent (I return to this point in Section 3.1.2) – content-independent in character. Understanding the character of such processes sheds light on how law is created and on aspects of those criteria of legal validity that law must meet in order to be identified and applied as law by courts and by other legal officials. Moreover, as I am keen to emphasise throughout this Element, exploring how the notion of content-independence can be transposed and used as an explanatory tool beyond the context of reasons for action, to inform and illuminate inquiries into law's modes of creation, identification, implementation, and application, is an area ripe for future research in legal philosophy.

3.1.1 An Objection Considered

Notwithstanding the points just made, some may question the scope and explanatory power of inquiries concerning the role of content-independence in the creation and identification of law, on the grounds that the earlier example drawn from UK parliamentary process is just that – one example – and that the points that can be gleaned from it are not generalisable beyond its specific context and may be tied too closely to one theoretical approach to understanding law's character. Important points can be brought better into focus from unpacking, and attempting to respond to, various aspects of this objection.

Even within the United Kingdom, primary legislation emerging from the Westminster Parliament is, of course, just one way amongst many of making law, and such legislation is only one type of law that is identified and applied in UK contexts. Other parliaments and assemblies with law-making powers exist, such as the Scottish Parliament and the Welsh Assembly,[5] while decisions of courts creating precedents are also a source of law, and various types of law-making in the UK can be authorised and effected by acts of the executive including delegated legislation and the exercise of prerogative powers. The activities of this complex web of interacting institutions also take place within and are subject to – in a variety of different senses depending on the institution involved and the powers it is purporting to exercise – a range of international treaties and agreements and their domestic law implementation mechanisms. Moreover, although the UK's Westminster Parliament may appear – at least in some constitutional interpretations – able to create legislation with any content whatsoever,[6] many other jurisdictions place explicit content-based limitations on their legislative institutions' ability to make valid law.[7]

Nonetheless, I contend that the notion of content-independence has powerful explanatory potential as regards our understanding of issues concerning the creation, identification, and application of law, and does so beyond the specific context featuring in the earlier example. Indeed, my working hypothesis, explored in various ways throughout this section, is that law-creation and law-identification practices in all jurisdictions have – in some way(s) and to some extent – a content-independent element to them. An important task for future research in this area, then, will be to explore whether and, if so, in what sense this is the case.

Taking the approach outlined in this Element, one way forward in undertaking this task will be to consider:

(1) whether various forms of law-making and law-identification that we encounter in various jurisdictions involve something functioning as a 'container' in the sense outlined earlier and in Section 2.1.3;

(2) whether those various forms of law-making and law identification allow for the creation of legal norms with a range of different and, in some circumstances, perhaps even contradictory content.

Although this research agenda cannot be completed within the confines of this Element, in the remainder of Section 3.1 I offer some ideas and considerations

---

[5] Details of these institutions and the character of and limits on their law-making powers can be found on the websites of the Scottish (www.parliament.scot/) and Welsh (https://senedd.wales/) parliaments.

[6] Understood in this way, the doctrine is often traced back to A. V. Dicey (1959: 40–41). For an updated and considerably more nuanced view, see Elliott 2019.

[7] See *Oxford Constitutions of the World* (https://oxcon.ouplaw.com/home/OCW) for reference.

that may assist those minded to engage with it in future work. To begin with, let us note that it seems at least plausible that various forms of law-making and law identification that we encounter in different legal systems do meet conditions (i) and (ii) above. As has already been indicated, in the case of legislative institutions, the 'container' is the law-making processes and procedures that count as making valid law in the institution in question. The legislative acts that emerge from those 'containers' can have a wide range of different content, and what makes them all into valid legislation is not the content that they have but the fact that they have emerged from a process that is counted as a law-making process in the relevant jurisdiction. As regards case law in a common law legal system where judicial decisions can establish legally binding precedents for the future as well as settling the instant case, the 'container' is the fact that the relevant court has so decided, and, depending on the history and development of the area of common law in question, and subject to the rules on distinguishing, overruling, and so on, the relevant court could have, and indeed may have at a prior point in history, decided in a way giving rise to a legal rule with a different content. What law-establishing judicial decisions have in common is that they are what the relevant courts have so decided and that, according to the legal system in question, what the relevant courts have so decided constitutes the law.[8] As regards legal systems where judicial decisions do not establish binding precedents as part of the law for the future, the fact that a previous court has so decided may have at least persuasive gravitational force as regards deciding a later case. Moreover, in legal systems where judicial decisions do not create new law for the future, those decisions are outside of the law-creation and identification processes under consideration here. Interestingly, some contemporary legal philosophers argue that in *all* legal systems and legal traditions, courts have at least a *pro tanto* reason to treat the fact that a previous court so decided as a content-independent reason in deciding a legally similar later case, and that so doing advances the pursuit of certain rule of law values (see Lewis 2021 for a detailed and thought-provoking discussion of this point).

3.1.2 Content-Independence: A Matter of Degree?

What should we make, however, of the point that, at least in some legal systems (and, as is explored later in this section, as is emphasised in distinctive ways in some approaches to understanding law), restrictions exist placing content-based limitations on the ability of various legal institutions to make valid law? Examples of such restrictions include clauses in constitutions and in bills of

---

[8] Exactly which part of what the relevant courts have decided constitutes the law is, however, a controversial matter – for discussion, see Horty 2011; Lamond 2005; Stevens 2018.

rights that prohibit the making of laws on certain subject-matters – such as 'Congress shall make no law respecting an establishment of religion, or prohibiting the free exercise thereof; or abridging the freedom of speech'[9] – or that render invalid any law or part of a law which breaches certain fundamental rights – such as can occur according to the operation of the Canadian Charter of Rights and Freedoms.[10] Here, too, we find an issue that should be regarded as ripe for future research, with one important line of inquiry being whether content-independence can be a *matter of degree*.

In Section 2.1.1 I noted that one intriguing suggestion featuring briefly in both Hart's and Raz's characterisations of content-independence is that it can be a matter of degree or, perhaps, depending on the context, that certain phenomena may be both content-independent and context-sensitive (see Hart 1982: 255; Raz 1998: 274–275; Raz 2001: 8–9). Raz puts the matter as follows:

> Many of the conditions that propositions must meet to be true legal propositions, and all the fundamental conditions of this kind, are that they were made law by content-independent processes or activities. Content-independent conditions are those that can endorse different propositions regardless of their content. Typically, they can endorse both a proposition and its contradictory, though this is not always the case, and there can be degrees of content-independence (make any law, make any law that does not violate human rights, make any law—regulation—necessary to the implementation of a fair rent act, etc). If a condition of the truth of a legal proposition is that it conforms with the demands of justice, for example, the condition is content-dependent: it depends (not exclusively, but among other things) on the content of the proposition. If the condition of the truth of a legal proposition is that it was endorsed by the legislature, then the condition is content-independent, since while the legislature's endorsement was probably motivated by the content of the proposition, it is itself an act that can give validity to propositions of varying contents. It is the act of endorsing the content of a bill, whatever it may be.
>
> Content-independence is, as I pointed out, a matter of degree ... (Raz 1998: 274–275)

On this view, jurisdictions which place content-based limitations on the ability of various legal institutions to make valid law should still be understood as having content-independent processes and procedures for creating and identifying law, but their content-independence should be understood as being a matter of degree. Exploring this possibility further may prove a fruitful area for

---

[9] See the Constitution of the United States' 1st Amendment (https://constitution.congress.gov/constitution/amendment-1/).

[10] See, e.g., *Schachter* v. *Canada*, [1992] 2 SCR 679; *M.* v. *H.*, [1999] 2 SCR 3.

future inquiry given its relevance to the issue of the explanatory power and scope of the notion of content-independence in law.[11]

This is so not merely in considering the question of whether the law-making and law-identifying process in all legal systems must be content-independent at least to some degree. It is also of relevance in considering a related issue: whether all general theories of law's character must, to be successful, understand and be able to explain certain content-independent aspects of law's existence and identification. The discussion so far in this section, including the examples I have drawn on and the theorists I have referred to, may give the impression that the explanatory power of the notion of content-independence is limited to approaches to understanding law with a legal positivist leaning. I want to suggest, however, that this is not the case, and to propose that another interesting future research agenda as regards content-independence in understanding law lies in investigating whether and, if so, in what sense *all* general theories of law's character must make room for certain content-independent factors as regards the existence and identification of law.

3.1.3 Content-Independence and Law's Existence and Identification

Future research on this topic would do well to explore further *the reasons why* it may be the case that all general theories of law's character must make room for the notion of content-independence. Although this task cannot be completed within the confines of this Element, this subsection offers some ideas in this direction and Section 3.1.4 explores where space for content-independent considerations may lie in a variety of theories of law.

Why might it be plausible that any general theory of law must make room for the notion of content-independence? The answer is likely to lie in the significance of the acts and decisions of legal institutions in determining what is required according to law. Morality, which is frequently and usefully compared and contrasted with law in a variety of legal philosophical work, does not emerge from, and is not identified, recognised, or enforced by, social institutions. There is – mercifully – no 'Ministry of Morality' or 'Morality Parliament' driving moral policy and enacting moral norms. If we are let down by our friend in a manner breaching the moral duties of friendship, there is no 'Moral Norms Tribunal' before which we may seek redress. This being so, in considering how, morally speaking, we ought to act, or how a friend ought to have acted towards us, we cannot appeal to the actions and

---

[11] Moreover, such explorations may lead theorists to consider the extent to which and the sense(s) in which certain aspects of law should be understood in a content-*dependent* way. This point is mentioned again towards the end of Section 3.1.4 and in Section 5.2 of the Conclusion to this Element. I am grateful to an anonymous reviewer for raising this point.

decisions of social institutions. To establish what morality requires and what ought to be done, we must consider directly what there is genuine reason to do, what it would be good to do. The existence and identification of moral norms is hence paradigmatically a content-dependent matter: we establish that we ought to do X by showing that it is good or valuable to do X.[12]

Things are different in the case of law. Wherever various general theories of law stand on the relevance of various moral considerations to the identification of law,[13] all such theories place significance on the role of legal and political institutions' actions and decisions in determining what law requires. That a given jurisdiction has a certain set of legal and political institutions, and the practices of those institutions – including their practices of creating, identifying, and applying legal norms – are regarded as highly salient points to be explained in general theories of law's character. This being so, one way in which law differs from morality is that establishing what is required according to law must involve, at least in part, establishing the relevant legal and political institutions that exist, the processes via which they operate, and what legal content may be inferred as having been created, identified, applied, and enforced as a result of their operations. Unlike establishing what morality requires, then, establishing what law requires cannot be done solely in a direct, content-dependent way, by asking which norms are good and ought to guide our conduct. What is required according to law is determined, to a significant extent, by establishing the past and present practice of legal institutions. Such past and present practice can be viewed as the 'container' (Adams 2017: 147) from which a range of different legal content can emerge.

3.1.4 Identifying Law According to Various Theoretical Approaches

The remarks already made indicate some matters which future research should address in examining whether and, if so, why all general theories of law need to make room for content-independent considerations in understanding law's creation and identification. These points come further into focus when we consider some examples illustrating the place of content-independent considerations in various approaches to understanding law.

As I indicated towards the beginning of Section 3.1, approaches to understanding law often classified as legal positivist in character seem obvious candidates for accounts of law which grant a significant role to content-independent considerations regarding law's creation and identification. According to both exclusive

---

[12] I am simplifying in various ways for the purposes of illustration, but the relevant contrast between morality and law should be clear.

[13] This is explored further in Section 3.1.4.

and inclusive legal positivism, ultimately, law is identified by reference to social facts such as the practices of parliaments and the recognition of courts and other institutions. Although for inclusive legal positivists the merits of a legal norm may determine its legal validity and content, this approach remains positivist in character because the merit-based considerations in question are relevant only if, in a given jurisdiction, some social sources implicitly or explicitly make them so, such that the existence and the content of the law are ultimately to be determined by reference to social facts (see Waluchow 1994 for an extended explanation of the position).

It is also important to note that, in both inclusive and exclusive legal positivist accounts of legal validity, the institutional processes by which law is created and identified may be content-independent only to a degree. On both approaches, for example, certain institutions may be empowered only to make law on certain issues, or required to refrain from making law on certain issues.[14] Moreover, both approaches can and do acknowledge that sometimes law's social sources direct legal officials such as judges to consider certain moral matters, such as the conformity or otherwise of governmental action or legislation with fundamental rights. Inclusive legal positivism and exclusive legal positivism differ, as regards this latter issue, on their interpretation of such directions and whether they always incorporate into the law of the jurisdiction in question conformity with the relevant moral principles as a condition of legal validity. Both approaches agree, however, that, ultimately, law is law because it emerges from, is recognised according to and so on, social sources such as the practices and processes of constitutional formation and amendment, and the actions and decisions of parliaments, courts, and other legal institutions. Such sources can create, recognise, and apply a range of law with a variety of different contents. As has already been highlighted, the social sources are the 'container' in Adams' terminology (Adams 2017: 147 and elsewhere) and law is created, recognised, identified, and applied – at least in significant part – according to the processes and operations of that container.

Legal positivism, however, is not the only approach to understanding law[15] which places significant emphasis on the idea that legal validity depends on

---

[14] The Scottish Parliament is an example of a legal institution required to refrain from making law on certain issues, or with certain content, including those that remain 'reserved matters' – see Scotland Act 1998, ss. 28–29 and Schedule 5, www.legislation.gov.uk/ukpga/1998/46/part/I/crossheading/legislation.

[15] I put things this way largely for convenience in the context of showing that the notion of content-independence has an important role to play in a variety of theoretical approaches. In fact, I am very sympathetic to a point made by both John Gardner (2001) and Leslie Green and Thomas Adams (2019) that legal positivism should be viewed as a thesis about one aspect of the nature of law, rather than as a complete theory of law.

social facts and social sources that are – to a significant degree – content-independent in character. This idea also plays a prominent role in some contemporary natural law theories. For example, in characterising the relationship between his own natural law approach and legal positivism, John Finnis contends that

> [l]egal theorists who present or understand their theories as 'positivist', or as instances of 'legal positivism', take their theories to be opposed to, or at least clearly distinct from, natural law theory. Natural law theorists, on the other hand, did not conceive their theories in opposition to, or even as distinct from, legal positivism . . .. The term 'positive law' was put into wide philosophical circulation first by Aquinas, and natural law theories of his kind share, or at least make no effort to deny, many or virtually all 'positivist' theses. (Finnis 2020: introduction)

This view echoes through many of his works (Finnis 1996, 2003, 2014) and is given specific expression in the form of Finnis's support for a test of legal validity that is legal positivist in character:

> The primary legal method of showing that a rule is valid is to show (i) that there was at some past time, $t1$, an act (of a legislator, court, or other appropriate institution) which according to the rules in force at $t1$ amounted to a valid and therefore operative act of rule-creation, and (ii) that since t the rule thus created has not determined (ceased to be in force) by virtue either of its own terms or of any act of repeal valid according to the rules of repeal in force at times $t2$, $t3$. (Finnis 2011: 268)

On such an approach,[16] legal validity is determined by reference to the social fact tests for the creation and identification of law recognised in a given legal system. As is clear from Finnis's characterisation in the quoted passage, such tests are significantly content-independent: both the acts of a legislator, court, or other legal institution and, more generally, the rules for law creation and law recognition operating in a given jurisdiction could vary enormously in terms of their content. What is relevant to legal validity is that such acts took place and that such rules were actually the rules in operation in the jurisdiction concerned.

Moreover, on Finnis's view, legal validity plays a vital role in law's ability to fulfil its normative point/moral purpose: reasonably to resolve co-ordination problems and so set the framework conditions for the pursuit of the common good and enabling persons living in political societies to flourish: 'natural law theory holds that law's "source-based character"—its dependence upon social

---

[16] See also the 'weak natural law' thesis of Mark Murphy (2006). A different approach to legal validity is taken by other contemporary natural law theorists, such as Jonathan Crowe (2019: chapters 7–9).

facts such as legislation, custom or judicially established precedents—is a fundamental and primary element in "law's capacity" to advance the common good, to secure human rights, or to govern with integrity'" (Finnis 2020: section 1). Posited human law, created and identifiable via significantly content-independent social facts tests, brings determinacy, clarity, specificity, predictability, and stability over time to human affairs (Finnis 2011: 267–270). These features of positive law enable the creation, implementation, and enforcement of structures of co-ordination in the service of the common good (Finnis 2011: chapters IX and X). The importance and the potential of the technique of legal validity in serving such morally valuable goals are also richly explored in detail and depth by other works in the contemporary natural law tradition, such as Maris Köpcke's *Legal Validity: The Fabric of Justice* (2019), as well as by works that seek to escape categorisation, especially categorisation in terms of an alleged legal positivism–natural law divide, such as Neil MacCormick's *Institutions of Law: An Essay in Legal Theory* (2007, especially chapters 2, 3, and 9).

Contemporary natural law accounts hence embrace and seek to bring out the moral potential in the significantly content-independent technique of legal validity. There are, however, approaches to theorising about law which seem to reject both the terminology and the substance of legal validity, and to repudiate the idea of law being created and identified according to social sources and institutional processes. Is there any room for the notion of content-independence in identifying law in such approaches? My view is that – perhaps despite appearances – there may well be, and this is another issue ripe for further research for those interested in the role of content-independence in the existence and identification of law. Examples of the approaches to theorising about law that I have in mind here include Ronald Dworkin's interpretivism (Dworkin 1986, 2006) and later developments such as the thought-provoking theoretical stances advanced by Nicos Stavropoulos (1996, 2012, 2021) and Mark Greenberg (2004, 2011, 2014).

On first consideration, Dworkin's theory of law may appear to run entirely counter to the idea that content-independent factors and processes play a significant role in the creation and identification of legal norms. As mentioned in Section 3.1.1, if we transpose aspects of Adams' container characterisation of content-independence (Adams 2017) to the context of law's creation and identification, then, in order to ascertain whether various approaches to understanding law make room for content-independence, we can ask (i) whether the relevant accounts of law-making and of law-identification involve something functioning as a 'container' and (ii) whether those accounts of law-making and law-identification allow for the creation of legal norms with a range of different, and perhaps even contradictory, content. In discussing legal positivism and some contemporary natural law approaches earlier, I suggested that legal institutional processes and techniques used to create and to identify something as valid law could be viewed as functioning as a 'container' in the relevant sense, and that such processes could validate as law a range of norms with very different content. Dworkin's interpretivist approach, however, rejects many aspects of this picture of law's operation. For Dworkin, true legal propositions are not identified by their relation to social sources. Rather, they are identified by a process of determining what emerges from the best moral and political justification of a jurisdiction's legal and political institutional practice in light of the moral point or purpose that such practice serves. A proposition of law is true and is to be identified as part of the legal content in a given jurisdiction if it is *justified*, and that justification depends on its content, on what legal rights and duties it bestows on and demands from us, and whether those rights and duties truly do flow from the best moral interpretation of the relevant community's legal and political practices and the values underlying and informing those practices (Dworkin 1986). These points are brought out well by Dan Priel:

> What Dworkin says here is that for law to create obligations it has to be legitimate; otherwise it only creates what has the appearance of obligation . . . But since we believe that law is capable of being legitimate (and only when it is legitimate it creates obligations), then just like in the case of morality, we must look at law's content in order to know whether it creates genuine obligations. If, for instance, the law of a state is illegitimate its demands for one's tax money are no more legitimate (and thus no more capable of creating obligations) than those of the robber who demands one's wallet. . . . To be sure, the way the money is demanded and the identity of the person (or body) who makes the demand may affect the determination whether the demand is legitimate . . . Nevertheless, one crucial factor in determining whether the demand is legitimate is *what* is being demanded. (Priel 2008: 13, emphasis in original)[17]

Additionally, Dworkin's stance would dispute even the division of issues into (1) law's existence and identification, and (2) law's justification, upon which the section structure of this Element rests, as in order to exist as a true legal proposition something must be justified. Dworkin also rejects the very idea of law being constituted by individuable, discrete legal norms validated according to any test or criterion of legal validity (see especially Dworkin 1977: chapter 2; 2006: introduction and chapter 8).

Where, then, might there be room for the notion of content-independent considerations or processes in Dworkin's account of what makes legal propositions

---

[17] In this passage, Priel is offering his interpretation of Dworkin's claim that '[j]urisprudence is the general part of adjudication, silent prologue to any decision at law' (Dworkin 1986: 90; see also Priel 2011).

true/the determination of legal content? In my view, the place to look for such room is in the role played in interpretivist accounts of law by legal and political institutional history and practice in the determination of legal content. For all the many and significant differences between Dworkinian interpretivism and other approaches to law's existence and identification discussed here, as Nicos Stavropoulos reminds us, this approach still acknowledges the importance of the facts of institutional practice in determining legal content, and seeks an account that explains, amongst other things, the relations between those facts, certain moral facts, and the legal rights and obligations that we have:

> Legal rights and obligations vary when certain institutional and other non-moral social facts vary; and cannot vary as long as such facts remain the same. The class of relevant facts most prominently includes *institutional practice*, the actions or practices of political institutions and ultimately the actions and psychology of the agents that operate within such institutions. . . . Your right is therefore contingent upon and varies with the actions and practices of political institutions. The task for theories of law is to offer an account of legal rights and obligations that explains these relations. Legal positivism is an account of legal rights and obligations that appeals, at the fundamental level, exclusively to institutional and other nonmoral social considerations. Interpretivism is a kind of natural law or 'nonpositivist' theory since it claims that, in addition to institutional practice (and perhaps other nonmoral social factors), certain moral facts necessarily play some role in the explanation. (Stavropoulos 2021: section 1)

The facts of institutional practice, of course, can and do vary both between different legal jurisdictions and within legal jurisdictions over time. Those facts can change and could have been different; accordingly, they seem capable of yielding as true legal propositions a range of different legal content. An issue ripe for future investigation, however, is whether the character of and the role played by the facts of institutional practice on an interpretivist approach can be understood in some sense as a content-independent 'container' as regards the identification of legal rights and duties. Moreover, there are different ways of understanding the interpretivist position. Another intriguing question could hence be whether there is *more* room for the facts of institutional practice to be understood as a content-independent determinant of legal content according to what Stavropoulos refers to as 'hybrid interpretivism', where 'institutional practice constitutes by itself part of the law; moral facts constitute by them-selves another part; and the final content of the law is some function of the two parts' (Stavropoulos 2021: section 1),[18] than according to what Stavropoulos regards as 'pure interpretivism', where 'institutional practice is one factor in the

---

[18] See also Stavropoulos 2021: section 3 for further discussion of the hybrid interpretivist view.

explanation but does not constitute any part of the law. Rather, morality and institutional practice both figure in the constitutive explanation of the law in the sense that the practice determines the content of the law as certain moral facts dictate and in virtue of those facts' (Stavropoulos 2021: section 1).[19]

The arguably deeper and more pervasive role of moral facts in determining both why and how institutional facts bear on legal rights and duties in the pure interpretivist view (on this point, see especially Stavropoulos 2021: section 5), as well as Stavropoulos's assertion that according to that view institutional practice does not constitute any part of the law, may cast doubt on whether there is a content-independent element to the identification of legal propositions in the case of pure interpretivism. On the other hand, as the quotes indicate, Stavropoulos also makes clear that institutional practice remains an important, indeed indispensable, ingredient in the process of ascertaining which legal propositions are true. Further questions for investigation hence readily suggest themselves: need interpretivism leave room for an explanatory role for content-independence in characterising the role of institutional practice on the hybrid interpretivist and/or the pure interpretivist view? What would be the point of or the motivation for attempting to ascertain the role, if any, of content-independent considerations in determining the content of law on an interpretivist approach? The discussion so far suggests that the motivation would be strongly bound up with the need to offer an adequate explanation of the connection between true legal propositions and the facts of past and present legal institutional practice. Moreover, as Stavropoulos is keen to emphasise, the normative relevance of institutional practice is central to interpretivist theories and provides an important justificatory constraint on a government's ability to use coercive force against its citizens (Stavropoulos 2021: section 5). As Stavropoulos (2021: section 5) puts it: 'It is not merely uncharacteristic but also impermissible for legal institutions to enforce some claim against a person, unless the claim meets the conditions of legality by being appropriately grounded in institutional practice.' This indicates the vital importance to interpretivist theories of law of explaining the role of institutional practice in determining legal content, and so again we can ask: might there be a valuable role for the notion of content-independence in aspects of such an explanation? We can also ask whether there is a place for content-independent considerations in the varying post-Dworkinian stances taken by Stavropoulos himself (for example, Stavropoulos 2012) and by, for example, Mark Greenberg (for example, Greenberg 2014). One concluding point to bear in mind here for those considering developing this research agenda in the future is the idea that

---

[19] See also Stavropoulos 2021: section 4 for further discussion of the pure interpretivist view.

content-independence may, as discussed in Section 3.1.2, be a matter of degree. If this is so, then different theories of law could feature content-independent elements and, indeed, content-*dependent* elements in different proportions in their characterisations of law, with Dworkinian pure interpretivism lying perhaps at one end of a sliding scale in this regard. Interestingly, this possibility has been canvassed – albeit in outline form only – by Raz in the course of discussing the differences between Hart's and Dworkin's accounts of law:

> Content-independence is, as I pointed out, a matter of degree. A central feature of Hart's explanation of the nature of law is that it is just about absolutely content-independent at bottom. That is the fundamental criteria for validity; those whose existence does not presuppose others, are almost entirely content-independent. . . . It is an equally central feature of Dworkin's account of the law that it is not entirely content-independent. . . . Dworkin's theory no less than Hart's leaves room for content-independent criteria among those determining what he calls "the grounds of legal propositions." In his most abstract formulations, this expresses itself in the role of the history of the legal system as an element contributing to the determination of its content. But his account of law emphasizes the importance of content-dependent determinants of its content. It is part of Dworkin's account that the theory of law makes the truth of legal propositions depend on values like justice, and an alleged value which he calls integrity. (Raz 1998: 275)

This also indicates another interesting possibility in terms of future research in this area: it may be fruitful to consider the sense in which we must understand certain aspects of law as being content-*dependent* in character, and to reflect on the differences between various accounts of law in terms of the place of and the role for content-*dependent* considerations within them. This may prove a fruitful lens via which to examine various differences but also commonalities amongst approaches such as exclusive legal positivism, inclusive legal positivism, interpretivism, and certain contemporary natural law theories.

Where does all this leave us in terms of the possibility of content-independence in law and in theories of law? The discussion here has shown that the notion of content-independence raises interesting issues and has application beyond the realm of reasons for action. Content-independence has a role to play in understanding aspects of law's creation and identification, and, moreover, it can have this role in a much wider variety of theoretical approaches to understanding law than may initially appear to be the case.

3.2 Potential

In addition to helping to illuminate our understanding of what law is, the notion of content-independence can also be useful in illuminating aspects of law's potential for good. As I have argued elsewhere, a successful account of law's character very much includes exploring such matters (Dickson 2022: chapters 7 and 8). In this section, I sketch several ways in which content-independent features of law can help law to realise certain values, with the aim, once again, of identifying and bringing into focus possible directions for future research.

3.2.1 Enabling Clarity and Public Ascertainability

Content-independent processes for creating and identifying law of the sort discussed in Section 3.1 play an important role in bringing clarity, determinacy, and public ascertainability to what law requires of those subject to it. The processes concerned are intended to enable legal institutions to yield a view as to what, according to law, ought to be done, which can be understood as the view of the institution concerned. Aspects of those processes are also intended to yield agreement following debate and disagreement, and so to move discussions about what ought to be done from the realm of policy debate, and of moral and other disagreement, to the realm of what is legally required and can be applied and enforced by legal institutions. When combined with the feature of law that both the identity and the place in the legal order of various legal institutions are publicly known – for example, that the identity of legislatures and of courts and fundamental aspects of the relations between these institutions' decisions are a matter of public record – these factors bring significant clarity and public ascertainability to the matter of which legal propositions are true in a legal system.

An example can help in illustrating these points. In the United Kingdom, the Abortion Act 1967 clarified, significantly extended, and put into statutory law the circumstances in which it is lawful to terminate a pregnancy in England, Wales, and Scotland.[20] Prior to the introduction in Parliament of the then-named Medical Termination of Pregnancy Bill in 1966, and during the parliamentary passage of that bill between June 1966 and October 1967, there was extensive moral, political, social, and medical debate on the issues that the bill sought to address. Campaign groups and medical professional bodies weighed in on various sides of the debates, public opinion was sought, reports were commissioned, and individual Members of Parliament expressed their various views.[21] An eventual final text for the bill was agreed upon, and then passed through the content-independent parliamentary process for enacting primary legislation in the Westminster Parliament: the bill was voted on and passed by a simple majority of those voting in the House

---

[20] See the UK Abortion Act 1967 (www.legislation.gov.uk/ukpga/1967/87/contents). For a summary of the legal situation in Northern Ireland, see Rough (2023).

[21] For a helpful summary, see Brooke 2002.

of Commons and in the House of Lords, and received the Royal Assent.[22] Bills which emerge as Acts of Parliament as a result of that process are counted as statutory law in the United Kingdom because they have emerged from that process, and not in virtue of whatever their varying content may be.

Moral, social, medical, and political debate in the UK surrounding abortion did not, of course, cease with the passing and coming into force of the Abortion Act 1967. Vibrant and high-quality discussion and critical analysis of both the Act (see, for example, Lee, Macvarish, and Sheldon 2018; Sheldon 2016) and the wider issue it regulates (see, for example, Bloomer, Pierson, and Estrada Claudio 2018; Greasley 2017) continue to the present day. But the content-independent process of the relevant bill passing the House of Commons and the House of Lords and receiving the Royal Assent in 1967 was a decisive moment in the regulation of abortion in the UK.[23] This process was the means by which wide-ranging and multifaceted policy debate was channelled into a statutory law that has, since that time, regulated the medical termination of pregnancy according to the statute's terms. The relevant parliamentary process acts as a kind of funnel by which views on all sides are channelled into the text of a bill that is then amended in further parliamentary processes; if sufficient votes for it are obtained in both Houses of Parliament and the Royal Assent follows, the 'output' of that process, the Act of Parliament, now governs legal regulation of the issue concerned. Moral, social, medical, and political debate continues, but it now concerns whether and, if so, in what ways to amend or supplement or repeal an existing law which regulates abortion according to its terms. Moreover, once the Act has been passed by Parliament and has entered into force, the law regulating abortion in England, Wales, and Scotland can be identified by ascertaining what has emerged from the relevant content-independent parliamentary processes. Someone considering terminating a pregnancy and/or a medical professional considering carrying out such a termination can ascertain what legal rules apply to the situation without having to learn about or enter into the wide-ranging moral, political, social, and medical debates surrounding this issue. Whatever different views are held by persons in UK society on the moral, social, and medical rights and wrongs of abortion, all can agree that the rules contained in the Abortion Act 1967 are law because that Act emerged from the UK's Westminster Parliament according to that Parliament's processes for creating statutory law. Content-independent processes and procedures such as the process of parliamentary enactment by which the Abortion Act 1967 became law in England, Wales,

---

[22] See Section 3.1.

[23] The 1967 Act has been amended once, by s. 37 of the Human Fertilisation and Embryology Act 1990 (www.legislation.gov.uk/ukpga/1990/37/section/37).

and Scotland hence bring clarity and public ascertainability to the issue of what is required according to law.

3.2.2 Concretising Matters

Legal rules emerging from content-independent processes such as the process of statutory enactment can also concretise and take a specific stance on matters which, absent those legal rules, would remain significantly underdetermined. Suppose that there are moral reasons to protect human health and safety that lead a polity to the point of legislating on matters such as speed limits and the priority of various traffic streams at junctions and roundabouts as regards vehicles travelling by road. It seems highly plausible that those moral reasons would not yield an exact answer as to the maximum miles per hour speed that should apply to cars travelling on motorways, or an exact answer as to which stream of traffic should have priority at roundabouts or junctions. Legal rules, however, can specify and publicly mark, for example, a particular speed limit as the one which will apply, for now, to various types of vehicle on various types of road in the jurisdiction in question. In specifying 70 mph as a limit for cars on motorways rather than 67 mph or 73 mph, road traffic legislation concretises and brings determinacy to that which is underdetermined by the relevant moral reasons. In so doing, it can improve various aspects of guiding drivers to drive at safe speeds: it gives drivers a clear limit to observe, enables the provision of clear signage on the motorways, and facilitates consistent and reliable enforcement by the police. The concretised standard counts as part of law because it emerges from the 'container' of, for example, the process of statutory enactment. This, of course, is just one example chosen from many possible such examples. Law's content-independent processes for marking something as legally valid frequently facilitate the concretising of otherwise underdetermined moral reasons and value considerations across a broad range of areas including many aspects of human health, safety and well-being, taxation, and education (for thoughtful further discussion, framed in terms of the normative point of legal validity, see Köpcke 2019: chapter 4).

3.2.3 Co-ordination Amidst Pluralism and Agreement Amidst Disagreement

A further point that builds on those raised in Sections 3.2.1 and 3.2.2 is that content-independent processes for the creation, identification, and recognition of law can facilitate certain sorts of agreement within contexts of significant disagreement, and can hence assist law in regulating important matters in diverse and pluralistic societies. To return to an example discussed earlier: persons with very different moral views on the permissibility of abortion both as a matter of principle and in terms of the specific circumstances under which any such morally permissible abortions should be carried out can agree that, for now, the matter in England, Wales, and Scotland is regulated according to the terms of the Abortion Act 1967, and that the Abortion Act 1967 is law in these jurisdictions. Such agreement is important in various ways. Although those who believe that the current law on abortion in England, Wales, and Scotland ought to be reformed or even abolished are free to argue and campaign to that effect, they agree that what they are arguing for is a change to the current legal settlement on abortion. That the Abortion Act 1967 is the current legal settlement on abortion allows medical services, including those provided by the UK's National Health Service, to be organised, co-ordinated, and made available according to its provisions. Agreement on what the current state of the law is, in the context of ongoing significant disagreement as regards whether and to what extent the law is as it ought to be, facilitates governance in contemporary societies with pluralistic and diverse views.

That law is created and identified in significant part *via* content-independent processes and activities also contributes to law's ability to bring about agreement in the sense of providing salient resolutions to societal co-ordination issues. For example, although people in political communities disagree greatly regarding taxation matters, there is a significant degree of consensus around the idea that some tax monies ought to be raised and redistributed to support the functions of government, maintain a national defence, and provide essential public services. Raising money from millions of natural and legal persons in an effective and consistent manner and providing for its redistribution on a national scale is not a task that can be achieved by individuals, small groups of persons, or charitable organisations. Law, as one part of the governance apparatus, however, can achieve this task: it can use legal rules to impose duties on large groups of persons and sets of activities to pay certain taxes, to put in place the machinery to collect those taxes, to redistribute them, to pursue those who fail to pay them, and to resolve disputes arising regarding those rules' interpretation and implementation. In the UK such rules are contained in an annual Finance Act supported by a vast and complex raft of taxation legislation.[24] These rules settle, for the relevant fiscal period, which taxes and duties are to be levied in respect of which activities and circumstances. They bring agreement and co-ordination to questions regarding who ought to be taxed and to what extent. In line with the points outlined in Section 3.1.2, they also determine, often in complex and concrete detail, what is underdetermined by normative considerations regarding our duties

---

[24] For explanation and commentary, see Maxwell and Syeda 2022.

to pool and redistribute resources in a polity, and they provide mechanisms of dispute resolution and enforcement in respect of those rules. That such rules are contained in Finance Acts and other statutes which are recognised as law because they have emerged from the content-independent process of being passed by the House of Commons and the House of Lords and have received the Royal Assent greatly facilitates the task of providing co-ordinative structures and concretised legal rules as regards matters upon which persons hold a wide range of moral and policy views. No matter where one stands on the morality of and the policy choices surrounding taxation, all can identify (sometimes, of course, with the assistance of a legally trained adviser) that the Finance Act and the many taxation statutes are law because they have emerged from the relevant parliamentary process, and can ascertain their duties by consulting that which has so emerged. Moreover, even where there is disagreement about the meaning or the application to a given concrete situation of aspects of various taxation statutes, there can be agreement as to which tax tribunals and courts are given jurisdiction by the relevant legal rules to resolve such disputes, and agreement as regards the status of the judgments issued by those institutions: namely that they are law because they have emerged as the decision of the relevant tribunal or court, rather than because of their content.

Similar points could, of course, be made regarding a wide variety of legal rules providing co-ordinative structures, concrete detail, and adjudicative functions in the face of widespread disagreement and normative underdetermination. That certain features of law – such as its use of rules to 'mediate between deeper-level considerations and concrete decisions' (Raz 1986: 58) and its capacity to bring about a certain kind of 'incompletely theorized' mid-level or low-level agreement in the face of disagreement at a more abstract level (Sunstein 1994) – can facilitate societally needed convergence, co-ordination, and concretisation has been identified as important and illuminated well by certain theorists (see also Köpcke 2019; Raz 2001; Sunstein 2018). Raz (2001: 18) contends that '[r]ules allow agreement in the face of disagreement. They do so by allowing for agreement on the decision procedure in spite of disagreements about the measures it should yield, or because of agreement on measures, in the face of disagreement about their justification.' Moreover, as is brought out in particularly rich terms by Sunstein, such methods can allow decision-making in pluralistic societies to take place in stages, and without the need for full agreement 'all the way down' to matters of first principle:

> Legal rules are typically incompletely theorized in the sense that they can be accepted by people who disagree on many general issues. People may agree that a sixty-five mile-per-hour speed limit makes sense, and that it applies to

defendant Jones, without having much of a theory about criminal punish-
ment, and without making judgements about the domain of utilitarianism and
the scope of paternalism. A key social function of rules is to allow people to
agree on the meaning, the authority, and even the soundness of a governing
legal provision in the face of disagreements about much else. (Sunstein 1994:
1741)[25]

My contention here is that an interesting future research agenda lies in investigating further the specific role of content-independence in contributing to these
features of law and, more generally, in facilitating co-ordination in conditions of
pluralism and agreement in the face of disagreement.

3.2.4 Advantages of Formalities

A further aspect of the potential value of content-independence in the context of
law creation and identification can be brought out by considering situations
where law empowers individuals to make legal arrangements for themselves.[26]
In the area of wills and succession law, for example, individuals are empowered
to make their own distinctive and binding legal arrangements as regards the
passing of their property and possessions after their death. The powers con-
ferred by law on individuals in this area have various aspects to them that appear
significantly content-independent. It is characteristic that various formalities
have to be observed in order to render a will legally valid, such as being in
writing, being witnessed by a set number of independent witnesses, being
signed by the person making the will, and so on. Such formalities do not refer
to or depend on the content of the will made according to them. A will made in
accordance with the relevant formalities is a legally valid will because the
relevant formalities have been complied with, and not because of the merits
or otherwise of the will's content. It is also a feature of wills law that, to
a significant extent, the testator can make a will with a variety of different
contents, all of which are legally valid if the content-independent formalities are
observed. It has been noted at various points in this Element that content-
independent conditions for the creation and identification of law can be
a matter of degree. This point has relevance here too: the overall framework
of legal rules regulating matters of wills and succession in a given jurisdiction
may include some conditions or exclusions of content, as is the case in jurisdictions where it is not possible entirely to exclude certain close relatives from
benefitting under a will.[27] In such jurisdictions, the conditions of a will being

---

[25] See Sunstein 2018 for a fuller development of his position.

[26] Hart 2012: chapter 3 reminds us of the importance of these sorts of laws.

[27] See, for example, the differences between Scotland and England in the rules on automatic
'forced heirship' in terms of legal rights of spouses and children. The main legal provisions

legally operative and binding are not solely content-independent in character. Notwithstanding this point, however, the power to make a will does enable one to make a wide variety of legal arrangements with different content, and many significant conditions of what renders a will legally valid are, as outlined already, content-independent. Indeed, arguably the freedom of self-direction to make a will with – to a significant extent – whatever content one wishes is very plausibly part of the point of conferring the relevant legal power on individuals (Köpcke 2019: chapter 5, section VII and chapter 6, section I offer thoughtful discussion of this and related points, as does MacCormick 2007: chapter 9). Additionally, once a will is validly made, it can be identified as such, and can endure as such through time unless amended or revoked, by methods which do not depend on its content. If made in accordance with the relevant formalities and other aspects of the legal regulatory framework concerned, then a will creates legal duties on executors and others to ensure that the testator's estate is disposed of according to its terms. This power to create, very largely on one's own terms, a binding and enforceable legal arrangement which can be identified and applied as such by the relevant individuals, officials, and courts irrespective of their view on the contents of the will or whether it was morally or otherwise appropriate to make it with that content is valuable for individuals in several ways. In addition to the relative freedom of testamentary intent and power of self-direction, it means that we do not have to rely on the goodwill of friends, relatives, and others who happen to be around after we die in order to have our wishes respected. It gives a standing and ascertainable character to our wishes in this regard that endures over time, and it enables us to retain control over matters that are important to us, including that property and possessions which we own are distributed in ways consonant with our own intentions and wishes.[28]

In both the creation and the identification of a legally valid will, then, content-independent elements have an important place and are part of what enables the legal power to make a will to facilitate and instantiate certain values. The wills example is, of course, just one example. Another interesting avenue for future research to explore, then, may be the role of content-independence in enabling a variety of private legal arrangements to realise certain values.

It should also be noted that, in the examples given in this and the preceding three subsections regarding what content-independent processes of law creation

concerning wills can be found, respectively, in the Succession (Scotland) Act 1964 as amended (www.legislation.gov.uk/ukpga/1964/41/contents) and the Wills Act 1837 (www.legislation.gov.uk/ukpga/1964/41/contents). For discussion of the past and present situation in Scots law, see Reid 2020.

[28] Various of these points receive detailed and thoughtful attention in MacCormick 2007: chapter 9.

and identification can be good for, I have largely focussed on the activities and legal output of legislative institutions. Although the current subsection does broaden things somewhat in considering individuals' powers to make legally binding arrangements such as wills, future inquiries could consider the issues raised in Sections 3.2.1–3.2.4 across a broader range of law-creation, law-identification, and law-implementation methods. Such inquiries might also usefully reflect on the degree of content-independence in various of those methods, and the relation between that and their aptness for contributing to law's ability to realise the relevant values.

4 Content-Independence in Law: Aspects of Justification

As noted in Sections 1 and 2 of this Element, many existing discussions of content-independence focus largely on what we might call its justificatory aspects: for example, whether and, if so, how there can be content-independent reasons for action (Adams 2017; Green 1988; Markwick 2000, 2003; Raz 1986) or content-independent justifications of rules (Gur 2011; Raz 2001), or the extent to which political obligation is content-independent (Klosko 2011, 2023; Valentini 2018; Walton 2014; Zhu 2018). In the context of understanding law, content-independence features heavily in certain theorists' accounts of the authority of law, both as regards explaining the character of law's claims to authority and as regards the conditions, if any, under which such claims could be true. As we shall see, in this context, the second characterisation of content-independence canvassed in Section 2.1.2 – the intentions as reasons characterisation – is particularly useful in bringing to the fore various puzzles regarding whether and, if so, how the fact that law requires something can function as a reason for action for those subject to it.[29] The first part of this section (Section 4.1) considers the relevance of the notion of content-independence in understanding various issues regarding law's claims to authority, and how those claims are viewed by those subject to law. In the second part (Section 4.2), I raise some possibilities regarding whether content-independence may make a positive contribution to law's ability to instantiate certain values and avoid certain risks.

4.1 Possibility

4.1.1 Law's Claims

A variety of legal and political philosophers view law as claiming to have authority (Edmundson 2002; Finnis 1984, 2011: chapters IX and X; Gardner

---

[29] Aspects of the 'independent of content characterisation' explored in Section 2.1.1 are also relevant to the discussion in this section.

2012; Green 1988; Raz 1986: chapters 2–4; Raz 1994a; Roughan 2018; Wolff 1970: chapter I). While there are some doubters regarding whether law is capable of making any such claims (Dworkin 2002; Himma 2001: 277–279), and as regards whether the claim law makes is a claim to authority rather than, for example, a claim to moral correctness (Alexy 2002), a strong case is made by John Gardner that legal officials, when acting in their capacity as such, should be understood as making claims to authority on law's behalf (Gardner 2012: 125–132). Many discussions of the authority of law, including the present one, adopt a kind of personification of the law, and speak of the law and of legal institutions making claims to authority. This personification of the law should be understood in a minimalist sense: as a shorthand way of referring to the claims that legal officials make on law's behalf (Gardner 2012: 132; Raz 1986: 70).

But what exactly is the claim to authority that law makes? Although they take very different stances on whether and when law actually has the authority it claims, a variety of theorists regard law as claiming that it has a right to rule which comes with a correlative duty to obey on the part of those subject to law (Finnis 2011: chapters IX and X; Raz 1986: 26; Raz 1994b: 341; Wolff 1970: chapter I). It is a claim that law possesses legitimate authority and hence generates moral reasons to obey it (Raz 2009a: 30–33). Moreover, law's claim to authority is regarded as general in character: it applies to all law in a given jurisdiction and not merely to specific areas of law (Finnis 1984; Raz 1994b: 341–342), and it is presented as *not* being dependent on the content of the law. Law's claim is that it ought to be obeyed because it is the law, not because of the meritorious content of a particular law or area of law (Christiano 2020: section 1.2; Finnis 2011: chapter IX.2; Raz 1986: 76–77).

It should already be apparent why the notion of content-independence is invoked by various theorists in their endeavours to understand the claim to authority that law makes. First of all, law's authority claim exhibits aspects of the 'independent of content characterisation' of content-independence discussed in Section 2.1.1. Law claims that those subject to it have reasons to follow it that are not directly related to the value of the content of its directives. As Thomas Christiano puts it:

> The commands of a legitimate political authority are usually thought to involve something more than this [the duty being dependent on the content of the command]. The duty of the subject is grounded not in the content of the command itself but in the nature of the source issuing the command. The duty to obey is then automatically generated when the command is issued by the appropriate authority and when it has the right form and provenance. In this respect, the duty to obey is content independent or independent of the content of the particular command. (Christiano 2020: section 1.2)

Moreover, when we ask 'If not in virtue of its meritorious content, then in virtue of what does law claim that we are obligated to obey it?', the answer – at least in part – is 'Because law said so.'. This, of course, resonates with aspects of the 'intentions as reasons characterisation' of content-independence discussed in Section 2.1.2. The claim that UK legal officials make on behalf of, for example, statute law emanating from the Westminster Parliament is not that those subject to those statutes ought to obey them because of the merits of their content. Rather, the claim is that they ought to obey because those statutes have been passed by the Westminster Parliament according to its law-making processes, and because when Parliament legislates it is intended that, and it is recognised by the courts that, the fact that Parliament has so legislated generates reasons for action for those subject to its legal directives.

4.1.2 Because Law Says So?

Owing to its importance in debates regarding the authority of law, and its relevance for the role of content-independence in such debates, it is worth digging deeper into the point that law claims (as indicated in Section 4.1.1, this should be understood in terms of legal officials making claims on behalf of law) that we ought to do as it requires not because of the merits of the content of its directives but because law so requires it. Many theorists understand authority claims, and the acceptance of such claims by some of those subject to them, in these terms:

> One must obey because one has been commanded and not because of the particular content of the command. One must do it because one has been told to do it. This kind of duty seems to be the most central kind of duty involved in the duty to obey. It is the idea that one must obey the authority because it is the authority. (Christiano 2020: section 1.2)

> Authoritative utterances can be called 'content-independent' reasons. A reason is content-independent if there is no direct connection between the reason and the action for which it is a reason. The reason is in the apparently 'extraneous' fact that someone in authority has said so. (Raz 1986: 35)

> The claims the law makes for itself are evident from the language it adopts and from the opinions expressed by its spokesmen, i.e. by the institutions of the law. The law's claim to authority is manifested by the fact that legal institutions are officially designated as 'authorities', by the fact that they regard themselves as having the right to impose obligations on their subjects, by their claims that their subjects owe them allegiance, and that their subjects ought to obey the law as it requires to be obeyed (i.e. in all cases except those in which some legal doctrine justifies breach of duty). (Raz 1994a: 215–216)

> [T]he fact that some action is legally required must itself count in the practical reasoning of the citizens, independently of the nature and merits of that action. (Green 1988: 225)

> Obedience is not a matter of doing what someone tells you to do. It is a matter of doing what he tells you to do *because he tells you to do it*. (Wolff 1970: 9, emphasis in original)

It is clear, then, that the 'because law says so' condition is frequently and, in my view, plausibly attributed to law's claims to authority. It should be noted, however, that it also gives rise to several important puzzles. One such puzzle is that, arguably, the better – morally speaking – law's directives are, the less plausible and indeed the less palatable it seems to become that we have 'because law says so' content-independent reasons for obeying them. As Raz puts it:

> Consider legal duties such as the duty not to commit murder and not to rape. Clearly there are moral duties to refrain from murder and from rape. Moreover, we expect morally conscientious people to comply with these laws because the acts they forbid are immoral. I would feel insulted if it were suggested that I refrain from murder and rape because I recognize a moral obligation to obey the law. We expect people to avoid such actions whether or not they are legally forbidden, and for reasons which have nothing to do with the law. (Raz 1994b: 343)

A second puzzle concerns the at best opaque character of the reason to obey the law allegedly supplied by the fact that law says so. As discussed in Section 2.1.2, the mere fact that some person or entity has required me to do something is not normally a reason for action for me. To mention again the example used in that previous discussion, if, while walking beside the River Thames in Oxford, I meet a colleague who says to me, 'You are required to jump in the river because I say so, and because I intend my saying so to function as a reason for action for you,' I do not regard this as creating for me a reason for action. Are things different with law such that the fact that law requires something, and that it is intended (as claimed by legal officials on law's behalf) that this fact will generate a reason for action, is somehow sufficient for such a reason actually to arise? If things *are* different with law in this regard then in what way(s) and in virtue of what are they different? This puzzle illuminates the way towards another: can there be reasons to obey the law *solely* in virtue of the fact that law requires certain things of us, or should the 'because law says so' condition be interpreted rather as a necessary but not sufficient condition of law providing reasons for action? As was also noted in Section 2.1.2, Noam Gur characterises this latter interpretation as 'the *weak sense* of content-independence' (Gur 2011: 180, emphasis in original) wherein the reason for action generated by law 'is not attributable to the mere fact that law requires the action. Rather, it depends on substantive factors' (Gur 2011: 180). As is discussed in Section 4.1.4, this sort of stance features prominently in certain accounts of how, and under what circumstances, law can be justified in its claims to provide us with reasons for action. As we shall see, in addressing this puzzle, different accounts take different views as regards which 'substantive factors' are capable of supplementing the 'because law says so' condition.

A final puzzle arising from the 'because law says so' element of law's claim to authority is that, on some views, accepting claims to authority inevitably involves an unacceptable breach of duties that one is argued to have, such as the duty to be autonomous and rationally to take responsibility for one's actions. According to philosophical anarchist Robert Paul Wolff:

> The defining mark of the state is authority, the right to rule. The primary obligation of man is autonomy, the refusal to be ruled. It would seem, then, that there can be no resolution of the conflict between the autonomy of the individual and the putative authority of the state. Insofar as a man fulfills his obligation to make himself the author of his decisions, he will resist the state's claim to have authority over him. That is to say, he will deny that he has a duty to obey the laws of the state *simply because they are the laws*. (Wolff 1970: 12, emphasis in original)

As is explored in Section 4.2.1, some theorists believe that the challenges raised by various of these puzzles can be overcome; others regard aspects of those challenges as insurmountable, leading them to embrace a view in which the authority that law *actually possesses*, rather than the authority that law claims, is limited or even non-existent. However, even those who reach the conclusion that law's claim to authority is never justified regard it as important to understand the character of that claim, and to examine the challenges it presents in terms of morality and rationality (Wolff 1970: chapter I).

4.1.3 The Need to Explain Belief in the Authority of Law

As the discussion in this section shows, the notion of content-independence, and particularly its relevance to the 'because law says so' condition, is useful in facilitating our understanding of the claim to authority that law makes, as well as in illuminating some puzzles that this claim gives rise to. It can also assist us in understanding the character of beliefs held by some of those living under law that law's claims to authority are true.

Many theorists take the view that one hallmark of authority is the ability to create directives that are – at least in some cases – binding even if mistaken, including if they are mistaken as to what, morally speaking, ought to be done (see, in addition to the quotations that follow, Christiano 2020: section 7.1; Gardner 2012: 142–144; Parry 2017; Raz 2017: 142, 159; Renzo 2019):[30]

> [L]et us examine the case of authority, using as our point of reference once again the idea of a content-independent command ... When a judge decides a case at law, she settles the dispute in a way that is binding even if wrong. (Green 1988: 56)

> [T]he thesis is not that authoritative determinations are binding only if they correctly reflect the reasons on which they depend. On the contrary, there is no point in having authorities unless their determinations are binding even if mistaken (though some mistakes may disqualify them). (Raz 1986: 47–48)

The notion of content-independence can assist in making sense of this idea: if authorities can create reasons for action which are reasons not in virtue of the quality of their content but instead in virtue of their source/the fact that the authority has decreed them, then space is made for the possibility of authoritative directives being binding even if wrong in terms of their content.

Certain theorists also draw attention to the point that some of those living under law accept law's claims and believe that legal directives can be binding even if mistaken. They contend that it is important in attempting to understand the authority of law that theories of law take it as part of their task to explain these beliefs and what it is to hold them (Green 1988: 60–62; Raz 1986: 28–37; Raz 2009b: 107). Raz emphasises that it is vital that accounts of law are able to explain such beliefs as plausible, as reasonable to hold, and as not involving irrationality (Raz 2001: 11; Raz 2012: 39 minutes, 40 seconds to 44 minutes[31]).

But why must legal philosophers explain how it could be plausible, reasonable, and rational to believe that legal directives can be morally binding even if mistaken and/or morally defective? This seems an interesting issue meriting further investigation. One view is that we must do so in virtue of the alleged ubiquity of such beliefs, the unlikelihood that so many people could be wrong as to the possible circumstances of law's bindingness (Raz 2001: 11; Raz 2012: 39 minutes, 40 seconds to 44 minutes), and, more generally, because it is part of the task of legal philosophy to understand how those subject to and administering law understand themselves in terms of law (Dickson 2022: chapter 6; Finnis 2011: chapter I; Raz 1994a: 237).

Once again, the notion of content-independence is helpful in approaching these explanatory tasks. According to the independent of content characterisation of content-independence, the usual content-based connection between

---

[30] For criticisms of aspects of this view, see Venezia 2020.

[31] This reference is to a public lecture, the Kellogg Lecture, entitled 'Sovereignty and Legitimacy: On the Changing Face of Law, Questions and Speculations' that Raz gave in 2012 (Raz 2012).

a reason and the action for which it is a reason is dislocated (see the discussion in Section 2.1.1 of this Element). Space is hence made for the notion that the reason for accepting law as morally binding and obeying it does not stem from the morally good content of the law. Moreover, as both the intentions as reasons characterisation (see Section 2.1.2) and the container characterisation (Section 2.1.3) of content-independence bring to the fore, the reason rather inheres in the source of the legal directives in question: that the law says so. If a cogent explanation can be given as to how the fact that a directive hails from a legal source can render it a reason for action, then we will be on the way to explaining the beliefs of many of those living under law as plausible and reasonable.

4.2 Potential

4.2.1 Justifying Law's Authority Claim

But is such an explanation available? This subsection explores some possibilities in this regard. In so doing, it begins to illuminate the potential of content-independence to realise certain values by considering its role in justifications of law's authority that reveal aspects of what law can be good for.

Wolff famously takes the view that the claims of legitimate authority made by governments and their law are never true. Accepting such authority claims means doing as law says because law says so. As mentioned in Section 4.1.2, according to Wolff, doing so would inevitably involve an unacceptable breach of duties that one is argued to have, such as the duty to be autonomous and rationally to take responsibility for one's actions (Wolff 1970: chapter I). In Section 4.1.2 I presented these points as posing a sort of puzzle for the 'because law says so' content-independent aspect of accepting law's claim to authority: how is it possible to do as some other entity requires because it requires it and yet remain autonomous and rationally responsible for one's own actions? Wolff, however, does not seek to unravel this puzzle in the sense of reconciling the various components of it with one another. Rather, he firmly embraces one pole of it and rejects the other: we should remain autonomous and rationally responsible for our actions by refusing to accept that law's authority claims are ever true: 'Insofar as a man fulfills his obligation to make himself the author of his decisions, he will resist the state's claim to have authority over him. That is to say, he will deny that he has a duty to obey the laws of the state *simply because they are the laws*' (Wolff 1970: 12, emphasis in original).

For Wolff, then, no values are instantiated in the circumstances in which law has legitimate authority over those subject to it because there are no such circumstances. Nonetheless, understanding the content-independent aspects of law's claim to authority is important to Wolff, for it is these very aspects, especially the 'because law says so' condition, that reveal what – in his view – is so problematic about accepting law's claims on their own terms,[32] and underline the importance of the values of autonomy and taking rational responsibility for one's actions.

Raz takes a very different view. For Raz, successfully providing a structure of authority that facilitates the realisation of values in our lives together in society is law's core moral task:

> It arises out of the law's character as a structure of authority, that is a structured, co-ordinated system of authorities. Authorities are legitimate only if they facilitate conformity with reason. *The law's task, put abstractly, is to secure a situation whereby moral goals which, given the current social situation in the country whose law it is, would be unlikely to be achieved without it, and whose achievement by the law is not counter-productive, are realised.* (Raz 2003: 12, emphasis in original)

Law's ability to provide structures of authority is, for Raz, central to its potential to realise moral goals. Moreover, the notion of content-independence is crucial to Raz's understanding of the authority of law and to his views on the valuable function that law can perform and on what allows it to be capable of performing it.

As is well known, according to Raz, the usual test for establishing whether law has legitimate authority is given by the normal justification thesis:

> The normal and primary way to establish that a person should be acknowledged to have authority over another person involves showing that the alleged subject is likely better to comply with reasons which apply to him (other than the alleged authoritative directives) if he accepts the directives of the alleged authority as authoritatively binding, and tries to follow them, than if he tries to follow the reasons which apply to him directly. (Raz 1994a: 214, internal footnote omitted)

Raz further contends that for an authority to be capable of providing the service to individuals of rendering them more likely to act in accordance with reasons that apply to them anyway by following the directives of the authority than by attempting to follow those reasons directly for themselves, 'it must be possible to identify the directive as being issued by the alleged authority without relying on reasons or considerations on which the directive purports to adjudicate' (Raz 1994a: 218). This point resonates with the issues discussed in Section 3.1 of this Element concerning the possibility of content-independent processes for the

---

[32] It should be noted that, for Wolff, it can be morally acceptable to do as law says, so long as we do so after having formed our own independent view that we ought to act thus, and do not do so because law says so (Wolff 1970: chapter I).

identification of legal directives. Here, Raz is claiming that the identification of legal directives must rest on content-independent processes in order for those directives to be authoritative and to be capable of playing the valuable role of mediating between people and those reasons for action that apply to them anyway (Raz 1994a: 214; for further discussion of this point, see also Vega Gomez 2005).

Moreover, as this discussion also indicates, for Raz, the idea of doing as law says 'because law says so' plays a vital role in authorities being able to provide a valuable service to those subject to their directives. In Section 4.1.2 I raised the puzzle of how the fact that law requires something can constitute a reason for action for those subject to it. Raz's answer is that it can constitute a reason for action because the benefits of authority can be had only if those subject to it do not act directly for the reasons that apply to them anyway, but rather identify and do as the authority says because the authority says so: 'The mediating role of authority cannot be carried out if its subjects do not guide their actions by its instructions instead of by the reasons on which they are supposed to depend' (Raz 1994a: 214–215). It should be noted, however, that on Raz's view we should not do as law says *solely because law says so*. We should do as law says because it says so *and* because its saying so and our ability to act on its saying so rather than by assessing our reasons for action directly for ourselves play a crucial role in the law of a state being able to meet the terms of the normal justification thesis. The values that can be realised by law being able to fulfil its moral task are, for Raz, a vital part of the justification of its authority. This being so, Raz's account seems to feature what Gur refers to as a weak sense of content-independence:

> by this understanding of content-independence, the reason is not attributable to the mere fact that law requires the action. Rather, it depends on substantive factors (other than the content of the legal requirement), viz. attributes that a lawmaking institution may possess, such as the fact that legal requirements in the relevant jurisdiction ensue from a fair and just decision-making procedure; or that the relevant lawmakers are well placed (relative to private actors) to determine what ought to be done in certain situations or domains of activity; or that legal authorities, due to their salience and enforcement measures, are apt to facilitate beneficial coordination between people; or other possible attributes of a lawmaking institution. (Gur 2011: 180–181)

As Gur indicates, although on this conception of content-independence the reason for action partly stems from the substantive value(s) that can be realised by having a law-making authority decide matters, the content-independent aspects remain intact because the substantive factors concerned are independent of the content of the relevant directives. This is, of course, a central plank in

Raz's account: the substantive values of realising moral goals that cannot be realised without a structure of authority are attainable only if legal directives are identifiable and can be acted upon without individuals having to weigh for themselves the reasons on which they are based.

The points discussed here indicate the tenor of Raz's response to the puzzle of how the fact that law says so can constitute a reason for action for those subject to it. They also provide the basis for Raz's response to the other two puzzles concerning the 'because law says so' aspect of law's authority raised in Section 4.1.2. As regards the first puzzle mentioned – that the better, morally speaking, law's directives are, the less plausible and indeed the less palatable it seems to become that we have 'because law says so' content-independent reasons for obeying them – the key point is that Raz's account of the scope of law's legitimate authority yields the conclusion that it is *limited* in character, that it cannot be established in the case of all persons and/or all areas of law, and that it is always less extensive than the authority that law claims (Raz 1986: chapters 2–4; Raz 1994a). Only where law can successfully meet the terms of the normal justification thesis does it have the authority that it claims. This being so, Raz takes the view that there are gaps in law's legitimate authority, and that in those gaps we do not, in fact, have reasons to do as law says because law says so – though we may have such reasons stemming directly from morality (Raz 1994b).

Raz views his account of authority as also being capable of meeting the challenge raised by Wolff that doing as an authority says because it says so violates our duties of autonomy and rational responsibility. Raz's view is that, when the normal justification thesis test of authority is met, following the directives of an authority rather than attempting directly for ourselves to follow the reasons on which those directives are based can actually enhance our ability to act in a rationally responsible way (Raz 2006: 1015–1020; Raz 2009a: chapter 1). Raz's account of authority is complex and has been subject to much critical discussion, and a comprehensive analysis of it cannot be offered here. An interesting future avenue of research, however, could involve more intense focus specifically on the role played by content-independence in enabling law to carry out moral tasks and to realise certain moral values.

Christiano offers a different kind of justificatory account of the authority of law, wherein content-independent aspects of democratic decision-making processes play a central role:

> The duties that are owed the democratic assembly are content independent and pre-emptive duties. They are content independent duties because each member has the duty, with a class of exceptions we will review in a moment,

just because the assembly has made a decision. The duties are pre-emptive because the citizen must put aside the considerations she initially planned on acting on in order to treat the rest of her fellow citizens with proper respect. The idea of equal respect requires, on this account, deference to the decision of the majority and not acting on one's own judgment when the majority disagrees. So the decision of the majority gives a reason to obey that pre-empts or replaces the considerations one might act on were there no majority decision. (Christiano 2020: section 7)

Several important points emerge from this stance in terms of the discussion in this section. Christiano emphasises the content-independent character of the duty to obey the decisions of an appropriately democratic body (for a full account of the conditions such a body must meet, as well as an extended version of his argument as a whole, see Christiano 2008). People have a duty to obey directives emerging from the decision processes of democratic assemblies because those assemblies have so decided, and not because of the content of their decisions. It should be noted, however, that Christiano nuances the justificatory power of content-independent democratic input in two ways. First of all, as with Raz's justificatory account of law's authority, Christiano's view exemplifies what Gur terms a weak sense of content-independence (Gur 2011: 180). To recap, according to such a sense of content-independence, 'the reason is not attributable to the mere fact that law requires the action. Rather, it depends on substantive factors (other than the content of the legal requirement), viz. attributes that a lawmaking institution may possess, such as the fact that legal requirements in the relevant jurisdiction ensue from a fair and just decision-making procedure' (Gur 2011: 180–181). Indeed, Christiano's view is a version of the specific example Gur uses in this passage to explain the sort of substantive factors which may combine with the fact that an allegedly authoritative directive requires something in order to provide those subject to that directive with a reason for action. For Christiano, directives emerging from the decisions of a democratic assembly have authority, and those subject to them have a duty to obey them (i) because the democratic assembly said so and (ii) because, in the circumstances of reasonable disagreement about what ought to be done in political society, democratic decision-making processes treat people's judgements and interests with respect, give each person a reasonably equal say in deciding, and so publicly realise the values of equal concern and respect for all citizens (Christiano 2004: 284–287; Christiano 2008: chapters 3 and 6).

The second way that Christiano's account nuances the justificatory power of content-independent democratic processes is by making it clear that it is subject to limits: there are circumstances in which the substantive injustice of an outcome overrides the content-independent reasons stemming from the fairness of a democratic process (Christiano 2004: 287–290; Christiano 2008: chapter 7). He takes the view that 'the very same principle that grounds democratic authority also ground limits to that authority' (Christiano 2020: section 7.2), so that if democratic processes deprive some of the population of their democratic rights (for example by disenfranchising them), or deprive them of certain of their basic liberal rights (he gives as examples the right to freedom of association and the right to choose and pursue one's own aims in life), then those processes no longer publicly embody the values of equal concern and respect for all citizens in a polity. As a result, the democratic assembly's authority would be limited in scope: 'To the extent that the democratic assembly's claim of authority is grounded in the public realization of the principle of equal respect, the authority would run out when the democratic assembly makes law that undermines equal respect' (Christiano 2020: section 7.2).

There are several aspects of this intriguing account that seem to indicate interesting ground for future research to traverse. Could the limits that Christiano envisages on the authority of democratic processes and institutions be understood in terms of content-independent factors being a matter of degree? Do we need to consider in more detail exactly what those limits are and whether they might extend beyond, for example, disenfranchising some of a population, to making it more difficult for certain parts of the population to register to vote and to vote? Exactly which basic liberal rights have to be violated, and to what degree, in order for the fact that a democratic assembly has required something to fail to yield a duty to obey it? In a book-length treatment of his view, Christiano does flesh out some more detail (Christiano 2008: see especially chapter 7), but some questions of the sort raised in this section remain, and in the fleshing out arguably still more are raised. Christiano argues, for example, 'that the provision of an economic minimum is necessary to public equality and that therefore a democratic assembly that does not do what it can to provide this thereby weakens its own authority' (Christiano 2008: 160). This clearly raises questions of what this minimum should be, how it should be provided, and what should be the consequences for the authority of law if the democratic institutions of a given polity fail to implement it. Exploring these questions further may also better illuminate the relations between the content-independent considerations of the fact that a democratic assembly has so decided and the content-dependent considerations of substantive value and justice in an account such as Christiano's. It would also be interesting to consider the relations between Christiano's view of the values that content-independent democratic processes can realise – especially the values of respecting diverse views and generating determinate outcomes in circumstances of reasonable disagreement in politics – and the points raised in Section 3.2.3 of this Element concerning the ability of content-independent processes of law creation and law identification to facilitate co-ordination amidst pluralism and agreement amidst disagreement.

4.2.2 A Beneficial Division of Labour?

The role of content-independent factors in the interaction between different legal institutions also has the potential to facilitate law realising certain values. As discussed earlier in this section (see Sections 4.1.1 and 4.1.3), taking legal standards as content-independent directives involves viewing them as binding not because of their content but in virtue of some other feature of them, such as because they emanate from an authoritative legal institution. Legal systems contain many such institutions, and, as a result of their relative places and roles in the system, and to the extent that directives and decisions emerging from them provide content-independent reasons for action, various legal institutions are under binding duties to follow and apply the directives and rulings of other legal institutions because they are the directives and rulings of those other institutions.

These are, of course, very familiar features of legal systems. Courts are under duties to follow and apply legal directives emerging from legislative institutions. Even in systems where some courts have the legal power to judicially review and overturn some of those directives, they are bound to follow the constitutional norms relevant to that process that have been formed by the operations of other legal institutions. Sometimes, in some systems, legislatures are under a duty to respond to certain court judgments by reviewing, amending, or repealing legislation. In systems where judgments of courts at certain points in the judicial hierarchy constitute binding precedent, courts are under a duty to follow the legally operative parts of the prior decisions of other courts. The police and other executive agencies such as tax officials or officials administering social security and benefits payments are under a duty, in applying the law to individual cases, to follow relevant legal directives that have emerged from legislative and judicial institutions. All this being so, when we consider the authority of the law in the context of legal systems, we immediately apprehend that law does not consist of a single authority. Rather, it is a structure of interacting authorities wherein legal institutions are under a duty to follow, that is, to be guided by, the norms and practices of other legal institutions. This means that legal institutions do not have free rein as regards the rules that they create and/or apply, and the decisions they take: they are always acting within a systemic structure of authorities where they have reasons to follow the directives and decisions of other authorities not because of the quality of their content but because they are the directives and decisions of other authorities.

These features of law result in what can be thought of as a beneficial division of labour between legal institutions and their functions. Institutions and the processes within institutions that *create* legal directives have a certain degree of separation from the institutions and processes that *apply* those directives to concrete cases, and from the institutions and processes which determine whether a purported legal directive is valid in a situation of – for example – constitutional judicial review. Even in situations where the same institution engages in more than one such process – for example, in common law jurisdictions, courts frequently both apply pre-existing law and make new law – the processes are differentiated by the role that content-independent considerations play in each. In identifying and applying pre-existing law, courts must establish what has been laid down in past decisions of legislative institutions and of courts at certain levels in the judicial hierarchy because they are the decisions of those institutions, whereas the process of making new law is not primarily focussed on establishing what other institutions have laid down, though it may involve establishing the limits on the law-making power of the legal authority in question, which may have been laid down by the decisions of other legal authorities.[33]

The differentiation of legal institutions and of functions within legal institutions outlined here is both demarcated and facilitated by the notion of content-independence. The duty of legal institutions to identify and to act according to authoritative directives of various sorts (including both directives setting substantive legal standards and directives establishing matters of jurisdiction, scope, and validity) emanating from other legal institutions supplies constraints on what those institutions can do and situates them within a network of interacting authorities. It also enables legal institutions, and processes within legal institutions, to develop various sorts of expertise and specialisation, thus enriching the operation of the legal order overall. The skills needed to think creatively and to develop policy and steer it through law-creating institutions are plausibly significantly different from the skills needed to interpret and apply to concrete situations myriad complex directives already laid down by another legal institution. Moreover, and as will be explored further in Section 4.2.3, this division of labour and differentiation of function between and within legal institutions can also help to reduce some possible risks which may arise owing to a concentration of power in too few institutions and/or in too small a group of persons.

---

[33] It should be noted that, despite these processes being differently constrained by content-independent considerations, we should not expect to find in the reasoning of courts a clearly bifurcated approach. The reasons for this are complex and relate to the character of interpretation in the context of authoritative directives. For discussion of these points, see, e.g., Raz 2009b: 107–122; 2009c: chapters 9–12.

These issues regarding the way in which content-independence in law can facilitate and support a beneficial division of labour of the kind outlined here are ripe for further investigation. Moreover, there may also be a link between these issues and the points raised in Section 3.2.3 regarding the contribution of content-independence to features and techniques of law which enable it to support decision-making taking place in stages, for example with each legal institution playing a role in determining different aspects of various matters to different degrees, and decision-making on controversial issues without the need for agreement 'all the way down' on matters of first principle, in the circumstances of societal diversity and pluralism.

4.2.3 A Range of Input and a Bulwark Against an Excessive Concentration of Power in Determining Legal Outcomes

The beneficial division of labour and differentiation of function between legal institutions outlined earlier also contributes to a situation where there is a wide range of input into the development, formation, application, and execution of legal directives by institutions and the legal officials who compose them. Legal systems exhibit considerable complexity as regards their institutional composition and interactions. Frequently, multiple different legislative, adjudicative, and executive institutions have the legal powers to create and to shape the application of legal directives, and to do so in ways that fulfil other valuable goals, such as enabling regional and/or national-level representation and decision-making within a state. Courts are often significantly differentiated: in terms of subject-matter specialisation; as regards their relative place in the judicial hierarchy; and in respect of which other bodies' norms and practices they have duties to check and review. As legal systems are composed of a range of different institutions with different functions and personnel, each constrained in their activities by the fact that they operate within a milieu of authoritative directives of other legal institutions, law is made, refined, interpreted, applied, reviewed, and revised by a considerable range and number of legal actors. This can enrich the breadth and depth of ideas which feed into the development and implementation of legal directives and can act as a counterbalancing force in respect of the risk of power being concentrated in too few hands with too narrow a range of interests, perspectives, and abilities. Moreover, as any given legal institution is situated in a web of other legal institutions whose authoritative directives and decisions bind and circumscribe them, no single institution or decision holds unlimited sway over the determination of the legal situation of persons subject to law. The multiplicity and the complexity of legal orders and of the interactions between the institutions which compose them hence seem capable of acting as a bulwark against an excessive concentration of the power to determine persons' normative situation according to law. Although these points remain, as yet, somewhat speculative in character, they may prove useful in indicating some matters that would benefit from further investigation and research, including consideration of whether these points may hold in different ways and to different degrees depending on the specific arrangements of particular legal systems, and whether they hold to some extent and in some ways in all legal systems.

4.2.4 A Vital Role for a Broad Range of Legal Professionals

The points discussed in Sections 4.2.2 and 4.2.3 lead to another: the complexity of legal systems with their interacting institutions each constrained by directives binding on them because they emanate from other legal institutions generates a need for a large community of legal professionals playing a range of roles. Most obviously, perhaps, the number and the complexity of different legal institutions and agencies engender a need for a well-qualified pool of legal officials to staff them, and to bring to the differentiated functions and legal processes of those institutions specialist expertise in creating, administering, interpreting, and applying the law. Also important, especially from the perspective of those living under the law, is the need for a well-qualified and professionalised pool of legal advice-givers able to assist with the task of understanding one's normative situation according to law given the complex interactions between legal norms and the institutions they emanate from. These latter would include solicitors, barristers, paralegals, and those offering legal advice from within charities, civic agencies such as the Citizens Advice Bureau in the UK, and employment law and tax law advisory services. Persons living under law must navigate a plethora of legal directives that are binding on them in virtue of having emanated from the relevant legal institutions, and in the context of those legal institutions themselves being constrained by authoritative directives stemming from other legal institutions. This gives rise to a need for experts in establishing what it is, exactly, that various legal institutions have authoritatively required, and how the totality of that which together they have required bears upon the legal situation of persons subject to law.

As Leslie Green reminds us, the growth and professionalisation of a specialist community of legal officials and legal advice-givers brings with it certain risks as well as certain advantages. Green alerts us to the fact that, because legal systems are necessarily institutionalised normative systems administered and enforced by a professional class of legal officials, law, by its nature, always and inevitably runs the moral risk of becoming distant from the communities it regulates, such that those communities become alienated from the law and regard it not as 'their law' but as something remote, imposed on them from without (Green 2008: section IV; Green 2012: xxix–xxx). Given the multiplicity and complexity of the legal regulatory environment discussed in this subsection and in the two which precede it, however, a professionalised community of legal officials and legal advice-givers to which people have adequate access is also much needed. Moreover, aspects of their professionalisation, such as their being subject to professional regulation, standards of qualification, and standards of professional ethics, can contribute to their doing a good job in helping people better navigate their lives under law. These features of law highlight for us the need to balance the relevant needs and risks in this area. A well-functioning legal system needs a large pool of highly qualified legal officials and legal advice-givers adhering to appropriate standards of regulation and professional conduct. But it must also take steps – some of which might plausibly feature in the relevant professional training – to try to ensure that these legal professionals do not become problematically distant from the communities they ultimately serve, and that those communities have proper access to the professional services they provide.

5 Summary and Avenues for Future Research

5.1 Summary

This Element has considered the notion of content-independence in the context of understanding various aspects of the character of law. As indicated from Section 1 onwards, 'the character of law' should be understood expansively, as encompassing both (1) inquiry into that which makes law into what it is and (2) inquiry into what law ought to be, which values it ought to serve, and which features of law may play a facilitative role in realising aspects of its potential. Section 2 of the Element began by outlining and analysing three possible characterisations of content-independence that might be relevant to the inquiry: (i) the independent of content characterisation; (ii) the intentions as reasons characterisation; and (iii) the container characterisation. Towards the end of that section, I began to explore the idea that which of these characterisations prove(s) to be apt and illuminating may vary according to the aspects of law's character and operation under consideration. Section 3 of the Element explored the role of content-independence in facilitating our understanding of aspects of the existence and identification of law. Matters highlighted by characterisation (i) – the independent of content characterisation – and by characterisation (iii) – the container characterisation – proved particularly apposite in this regard. A central contention of Section 3, and indeed of the Element as a whole, is that we should explore further the idea of content-independence not only as regards the possible existence and character of content-independent reasons for action but in terms of what it can help us to understand regarding law's existence as a social, institutional, and systemic phenomenon. Notwithstanding this contention, the notion of content-independence does have a useful role to play in understanding the character of reasons for action of the sort that law claims to be able to provide. Section 4 of the Element approached some of the relevant issues via an exploration of aspects of law's claim to authority, especially the 'because law says so' component of it. Aspects of characterisation (ii) – the intentions as reasons characterisation of content-independence – were useful in illuminating various relevant issues, as were aspects of (i) – the independent of reasons characterisation. Both Sections 3 and 4 of this Element closed by considering the potential of the notion of content-independence in facilitating law's ability to realise certain values and in attempting to ameliorate certain risks.

5.2 Avenues for Future Research

One important aim of the Cambridge Elements in Philosophy of Law series is to bring into focus fresh research agendas for the future. I have sought to do this throughout this Element and conclude it by summarising the suggestions made in each section as regards potentially fruitful avenues for future research to explore. Where the same suggestion is repeated in different sections, I list it only under the section in which it first appears.

Section 2:
- A shift in focus as regards which aspects of content-independence future research focusses on, in order for this notion to illuminate a broader range of questions regarding law beyond existing studies that focus largely on content-independent reasons for action (Section 2: introduction).
- Further consideration of the character and role of a 'container' (Adams 2017) in the container characterisation of content-independence (Section 2.1.3).
- Further consideration of the relations between the three characterisations of content-independence discussed in this section, and whether any other characterisation is plausible and useful (Section 2.2).

Section 3:
- What the notion of content-independence can help us to understand regarding law's existence as a social, institutional, and systemic phenomenon (Section 3: introduction).

- Whether all forms of law creation and law identification in all jurisdictions have – in some way(s) and to some extent – a content-independent element to them (Section 3.1.1).
- Whether and, if so, in what sense content-independence can be a matter of degree (Section 3.1.2).
- Whether and, if so, to what extent, in what ways, and why the notion of content-independence must feature in any successful general theory of the character of law (Sections 3.1.3–3.1.4).
- The extent to which, and the senses in which, aspects of law must be understood in content-*dependent* ways (Section 3.1.4).
- Whether the place of and the role for content-*dependent* considerations in theories of law may be an interesting lens via which to consider both differences and commonalities as regards various approaches to understanding law (Section 3.1.4).
- Further consideration of various of the ways in which content-independent processes and conditions as regards the existence and identification of law can help law to realise certain values, including facilitating the clarity and public ascertainability of what law requires; concretising underdetermined moral matters; facilitating co-ordination amidst pluralism and agreement amidst disagreement; and facilitating individuals' powers of self-direction via the use of content-independent legal formalities (Section 3.2).
- Consideration of the potential of content-independent processes to help law realise certain values beyond the context of legislative institutions (Section 3.2.4).

Section 4:
- Whether and, if so, why legal philosophers must explain how it could be plausible, reasonable, and rational to believe that legal directives can be morally binding even if mistaken and/or morally defective, and the relevance of the notion of content-independence in reaching such an explanation (Section 4.1.3).
- Further focus on various aspects of the role of content-independent considerations in the justificatory aspects of various accounts of the authority of law, such as those offered by Raz, Christiano, and other theorists whose accounts may be particularly illuminating in this regard (Section 4.2.1).
- Further consideration of the relations between Christiano's view of the values that content-independent democratic processes can realise – especially the values of respecting diverse views and generating determinate outcomes in circumstances of reasonable disagreement in politics – and the point raised in Section 3.2.3 of this Element concerning the ability of content-independent

law-identification processes to realise the values of co-ordination amidst pluralism and agreement amidst disagreement (Sections 3.2.3 and 4.2.1).

- Consideration of the way in which the notion of content-independence in law can facilitate and support a beneficial division of labour between and within legal institutions (Section 4.2.2).

- Whether there may be a link between the issue of supporting a beneficial division of labour between and within legal institutions and the topic explored in Section 3.2.3 regarding the contribution of content-independence to features and techniques of law which facilitate decision-making taking place in stages, and facilitate decision-making on controversial issues without the need for agreement 'all the way down' on matters of first principle, in the circumstances of societal diversity and pluralism (Section 4.2.2).

- Further reflection on the role of content-independence in enabling and sustaining complex legal systems with a wide range of institutions which are mutually circumscribing and constraining and hence seem capable of acting as a bulwark against an excessive concentration of the power to determine persons' normative situation according to law (Section 4.2.3).

- Further consideration of the relations between the existence and operation of multiple, complex legal institutions bound by content-independent legal directives and the role of a professionalised community of legal professionals, including reflection on the role of the latter in realising certain values in law and in ameliorating certain risks that the existence of law engenders (Section 4.2.4).

It is my hope that this Element will stimulate interest in, and help to illuminate aspects of, these and other fresh research agendas.

References

Adams, N. P. (2017). 'In Defense of Content-Independence'. *Legal Theory* 23: 143–167.

Alexy, R. (2002). *The Argument from Injustice: A Reply to Legal Positivism.* Oxford: Clarendon Press.

Bloomer, F., Pierson, C., and Estrada Claudio, S. (2018). *Reimagining Global Abortion Politics: A Social Justice Perspective.* Bristol: Policy Press.

Brooke, S. (2002). 'Abortion Law Reform 1929–69' in Institute of Contemporary British History Witness Seminar 2002, 'The Abortion Act 1967', held 10 July 2001, www.kcl.ac.uk/sspp/assets/icbh-witness/abortionact1967.pdf, 15–20.

Christiano, T. (2004). 'The Authority of Democracy'. *Journal of Political Philosophy* 12: 266–290.

Christiano, T. (2008). *The Constitution of Equality: Democratic Authority and Its Limits.* Oxford: Oxford University Press.

Christiano, T. (2020). 'Authority' in Zalta, E. (ed.), *The Stanford Encyclopedia of Philosophy* (summer 2020 ed.). https://plato.stanford.edu/archives/sum2020/entries/authority/.

Coleman, J. L. (2001). *The Practice of Principle: In Defence of a Pragmatist Approach to Legal Theory.* Oxford: Oxford University Press.

Crowe, J. (2019). *Natural Law and the Nature of Law.* Cambridge: Cambridge University Press.

Dagger, R., and Lefkowitz, D. (2021). 'Political Obligation' in Zalta, E. (ed.), *The Stanford Encyclopedia of Philosophy* (summer 2021 ed.). https://plato.stanford.edu/archives/sum2021/entries/political-obligation/.

Dicey, A. V. (1959). *The Law of the Constitution*, 10th ed. (ed. E. C. S. Wade). London: Macmillan.

Dickson, J. (2015). 'Ours Is a Broad Church: Indirectly Evaluative Legal Philosophy as a Facet of Jurisprudential Inquiry'. *Jurisprudence* 6: 207–230.

Dickson, J. (2022). *Elucidating Law.* Oxford: Oxford University Press.

Duff, R. A. (1998). 'Inclusion and Exclusion: Citizens, Subjects and Outlaws' in Freeman, M. D. A. (ed.), *Current Legal Problems* 51: 241–266. https://doi.org/10.1093/clp/51.1.241.

Dworkin, R. (1977). *Taking Rights Seriously.* Cambridge, MA: Harvard University Press.

Dworkin, R. (1986). *Law's Empire.* London: Fontana Press.

Dworkin, R. (2002). 'Thirty Years On'. *Harvard Law Review* 115: 1655–1688.

Dworkin, R. (2006). *Justice in Robes*. Cambridge, MA: Harvard University Press.

Edmundson, W. A. (2002). 'Social Meaning, Compliance Conditions, and Law's Claim to Authority'. *Canadian Journal of Law and Jurisprudence* 15: 51–67.

Elliott, M. (2019). 'Parliamentary Sovereignty in a Changing Constitutional Landscape', in O'Cinneide, C., and Jowell, J. (eds.), *The Changing Constitution*, 9th ed. Oxford: Oxford University Press, 29–57.

Finnis, J. (1984). 'The Authority of Law in the Predicament of Contemporary Social Theory'. *Notre Dame Journal of Law, Ethics and Public Policy* 1: 115–138.

Finnis, J. (1996). 'The Truth in Legal Positivism' in George, R. (ed.), *The Autonomy of Law: Essays on Legal Positivism*. Oxford: Oxford University Press, 195–214.

Finnis, J. (2003). 'Law and What I Truly Should Decide', *American Journal of Jurisprudence* 48: 107–129.

Finnis, J. (2011). *Natural Law and Natural Rights*, 2nd ed. Oxford: Clarendon Press.

Finnis, J. (2014). 'What Is the Philosophy of Law?', *American Journal of Jurisprudence* 59: 133–142.

Finnis, J. (2020). 'Natural Law Theories' in Zalta, E. (ed.), *The Stanford Encyclopedia of Philosophy* (summer 2020 ed.). https://plato.stanford.edu/archives/sum2020/entries/natural-law-theories/#.

Flanigan, E. T. (2020). 'Do We Have Reasons to Obey the Law?'. *Journal of Ethics and Social Philosophy* 17(2): 159–197.

Gardner, J. (2001). 'Legal Positivism: 5½ Myths'. *American Journal of Jurisprudence* 46: 199–227.

Gardner, J. (2007). 'Nearly Natural Law'. *American Journal of Jurisprudence* 52: 1–23.

Gardner, J. (2012). 'How Law Claims, What Law Claims' in Gardner, J., *Law as a Leap of Faith*. Oxford: Oxford University Press, 125–148.

Giudice, M. (2008). 'The Regular Practice of Morality in Law'. *Ratio Juris* 21: 94–106.

Greasley, K. (2017). *Arguments About Abortion: Personhood, Morality, and Law*. Oxford: Oxford University Press.

Green, L. (1988). *The Authority of the State*. Oxford: Clarendon Press.

Green, L. (2008). 'Positivism and the Inseparability of Law and Morals'. *New York University Law Review* 83: 1035–1058.

Green, L. (2012). 'Introduction' in Hart, H. L. A., *The Concept of Law*, 3rd ed. Oxford: Oxford University Press, xv–lv.

Green, L. (2023). *The Germ of Justice: Essays in General Jurisprudence*. Oxford: Oxford University Press.

Green, L., and Adams, T. (2019). 'Legal Positivism' in Zalta, E. (ed.), *The Stanford Encyclopedia of Philosophy* (winter 2019 ed.). https://plato.stanford.edu/archives/win2019/entries/legal-positivism/.

Greenberg, M. (2004). 'How Facts Make Law'. *Legal Theory* 10: 157–198.

Greenberg, M. (2011). 'The Standard Picture and Its Discontents' in Green, L., and Leiter, B. (eds.), *Oxford Studies in Philosophy of Law: Volume 1*. Oxford: Oxford University Press, 39–104.

Greenberg, M. (2014). 'The Moral Impact Theory of Law'. *Yale Law Journal* 123: 1288–1342.

Gur, N. (2011). 'Are Legal Rules Content-Independent Reasons?'. *Problema* 5: 175–210.

Hart, H. L. A. (1958). 'Legal and Moral Obligation' in Melden, A. I. (ed.), *Essays in Moral Philosophy*. Seattle: University of Washington Press, 82–107.

Hart, H. L. A. (1982). 'Commands and Authoritative Legal Reasons' in Hart, H. L. A., *Essays on Bentham*. Oxford: Oxford University Press, 243–268.

Hart, H. L. A. (2012). *The Concept of Law*, 3rd ed. Oxford: Oxford University Press.

Himma, K. E. (2001). 'Law's Claim of Legitimate Authority' in Coleman, J. L. (ed.), *Hart's Postscript*. Oxford: Oxford University Press, 271–309.

Himma, K. E. (2005). 'Final Authority to Bind with Moral Mistakes: On the Explanatory Potential of Inclusive Legal Positivism'. *Law and Philosophy* 24: 1–45.

Horty, J. (2011). 'Rules and Reasons in the Theory of Precedent'. *Legal Theory* 17: 1–33.

Klosko, G. (2011). 'Are Political Obligations Content Independent?'. *Political Theory* 39: 498–523.

Klosko, G. (2023). 'Content Independence and Political Obligation: Scope Limitations of Content-Independent Moral Reasons'. *Political Studies* 71(1): 30–46.

Köpcke, M. (2019). *Legal Validity: The Fabric of Justice*. London: Bloomsbury Press.

Kramer, M. (1999). *In Defense of Legal Positivism*. Oxford: Oxford University Press.

Kramer, M. (2004). *Where Law and Morality Meet*. Oxford: Oxford University Press.

Lamond, G. (2005). 'Do Precedents Create Rules?'. *Legal Theory* 11: 1–26.

Lee, E., Macvarish J., and Sheldon, S. (2018). 'The 1967 Abortion Act Fifty Years On: Abortion, Medical Authority and the Law Revisited'. *Social Science and Medicine* 212: 26–32.

Lewis, S. (2021). 'Precedent and the Rule of Law'. *Oxford Journal of Legal Studies* 41: 873–898.

MacCormick, N. (2007). *Institutions of Law: An Essay in Legal Theory.* Oxford: Oxford University Press.

Markwick, P. (2000). 'Law and Content-Independent Reasons'. *Oxford Journal of Legal Studies* 20: 579–596.

Markwick, P. (2003). 'Independent of Content'. *Legal Theory* 9: 43–61.

Marmor, A. (1995). 'Authorities and Persons'. *Legal Theory* 1: 337–359.

Marmor, A. (2001). *Positive Law and Objective Values.* Oxford: Oxford University Press.

Marmor, A. (2006). 'Legal Positivism: Still Descriptive and Morally Neutral'. *Oxford Journal of Legal Studies* 26: 683–704.

Maxwell, S., and Syeda, M. (2022). *Tolley's Tax Guide 2022–23.* London: Tolley from LexisNexis.

Murphy, M. C. (2006). *Natural Law in Jurisprudence and Politics.* Cambridge: Cambridge University Press.

Parry, J. (2017). 'Authority and Harm' in Sobel, D., Vallentyne, P., and Wall, S. (eds.), *Oxford Studies in Political Philosophy, Volume 3.* Oxford: Oxford University Press, 252–278.

Priel, D. (2008). 'Book Review: *Justice in Robes* by Ronald Dworkin (2006)'. All Papers No. 255, Osgoode Hall Law School of York University. http://digitalcommons.osgoode.yorku.ca/all_papers/255.

Priel, D. (2011). 'The Place of Legitimacy in Legal Theory'. *McGill Law Journal* 57: 1–36.

Raz, J. (1986). *The Morality of Freedom.* Oxford: Clarendon Press.

Raz, J. (1994a). 'Authority, Law, and Morality' in Raz, J., *Ethics in the Public Domain: Essays in the Morality of Law and Politics.* Oxford: Clarendon Press, 210–237.

Raz, J. (1994b). 'The Obligation to Obey: Revision and Tradition' in Raz, J., *Ethics in the Public Domain: Essays in the Morality of Law and Politics.* Oxford: Clarendon Press, 341–354.

Raz, J. (1998). 'Two Views of the Nature of the Theory of Law: A Partial Comparison'. *Legal Theory* 4: 249–282.

Raz, J. (1999). *Practical Reason and Norms,* 2nd ed. Oxford: Oxford University Press.

Raz, J. (2001). 'Reasoning with Rules'. *Current Legal Problems* 54: 1–18.

Raz, J. (2003). 'About Morality and the Nature of Law'. *American Journal of Jurisprudence* 48: 1–15.

Raz, J. (2004). 'Incorporation by Law'. *Legal Theory* 10: 1–17.

Raz, J. (2006). 'The Problem of Authority: Revisiting the Service Conception'. *Minnesota Law Review* 90: 1003–1044.

Raz, J. (2007). 'The Argument from Justice, or How Not to Reply to Legal Positivism' in Pavlakos, G. (ed.), *Law, Rights and Discourse: The Legal Philosophy of Robert Alexy*. Oxford: Hart, 17–36.

Raz, J. (2009a). *The Authority of Law: Essays on Law and Morality*, 2nd ed. Oxford: Oxford University Press.

Raz, J. (2009b). 'On the Nature of Law' in Raz, J., *Between Authority and Interpretation*. Oxford: Oxford University Press, 91–125.

Raz, J. (2009c). *Between Authority and Interpretation*. Oxford: Oxford University Press.

Raz, J. (2012). 'Sovereignty and Legitimacy: On the Changing Face of Law, Questions and Speculations'. Second Frederic R. and Molly S. Kellogg Biennial Lecture in Jurisprudence. www.youtube.com/watch?v=VMC9u7PZZCo.

Raz, J. (2017). 'Why the State?' in Roughan, N., and Halpin, A. (eds.), *In Pursuit of Pluralist Jurisprudence*. Cambridge: Cambridge University Press, 136–162.

Reid, K. G. C. (2020). 'Legal Rights in Scotland' in Reid, K. G. C, de Waal, M. J., and Zimmermann, R. (eds.), *Comparative Succession Law: Volume III: Mandatory Family Protection*. Oxford: Oxford University Press, 417–449.

Renzo, M. (2019). 'Political Authority and Unjust Wars'. *Philosophy and Phenomenological Research* 99: 336–357.

Rough, E. (2023). 'Abortion in Northern Ireland: Recent Changes to the Legal Framework'. Research briefing, 6 February. London: UK Parliament, House of Commons Library. https://commonslibrary.parliament.uk/research-briefings/cbp-8909/.

Roughan, N. (2018). 'The Official Point of View and the Official Claim to Authority'. *Oxford Journal of Legal Studies* 38: 191–216.

Sciaraffa, S. (2009). 'On Content-Independent Reasons: It's Not in the Name'. *Law and Philosophy* 28: 233–260.

Shapiro, S. (2000). 'Law, Morality and the Guidance of Conduct'. *Legal Theory* 6: 127–170.

Shapiro, S. (2002). 'Authority' in Coleman, J., Himma, K., and Shapiro, S. (eds.), *The Oxford Handbook of Jurisprudence and Philosophy of Law*. Oxford: Oxford University Press, 382–439.

Shapiro, S. (2009). 'Was Inclusive Legal Positivism Founded on a Mistake?'. *Ratio Juris* 22: 326–338.

Shapiro, S. (2011). *Legality.* Cambridge, MA: Harvard University Press.

Sheldon, S. (2016). 'The Decriminalisation of Abortion: An Argument for Modernisation'. *Oxford Journal of Legal Studies* 36: 334–365.

Stavropoulos, N. (1996). *Objectivity in Law.* Oxford: Clarendon Press.

Stavropoulos, N. (2012). 'Obligations, Interpretivism and the Legal Point of View' in Marmor, A. (ed.), *The Routledge Companion to Philosophy of Law.* New York: Routledge, 76–92.

Stavropoulos, N. (2021). 'Legal Interpretivism' in Zalta, E. (ed.), *The Stanford Encyclopedia of Philosophy* (spring 2021 ed.). https://plato.stanford.edu/archives/spr2021/entries/law-interpretivist/.

Stevens, K. (2018). 'Reasoning by Precedent – Between Rules and Analogies'. *Legal Theory* 24: 216–254.

Sunstein, C. (1994). 'Incompletely Theorized Agreements'. *Harvard Law Review* 108: 1733–1772.

Sunstein, C. (2018). *Legal Reasoning and Political Conflict*, 2nd ed. Oxford: Oxford University Press.

Valentini, L. (2018). 'The Content-Independence of Political Obligation: What It Is and How to Test It'. *Legal Theory* 24: 135–157.

Vega Gomez, J. (2005). 'Putting the Sources Thesis in Its Place'. *Analisi e Diritto: Ricerche di Giurisprudenza Analitica* 2005: 145–153. http://dx.doi.org/10.2139/ssrn.2789125.

Venezia, L. (2020). 'Mistaken Authority and Obligation'. *Legal Theory* 26: 338–351.

Walton, K. (2014). 'The Content-Independence of Political Obligations: A Response to Klosko'. *Political Theory* 42: 218–222.

Waluchow, W. (1994). *Inclusive Legal Positivism.* Oxford: Oxford University Press.

Wolff, R. P. (1970). *In Defense of Anarchism.* New York: Harper and Row.

Zhu, J. (2018). 'Content-Independence and Natural-Duty Theories of Political Obligation'. *Philosophy and Social Criticism* 44(1): 61–80.

Acknowledgements

I would like to thank Sebastian Lewis, Andreas Vassiliou, and the anonymous peer reviewers for the Cambridge Elements in Philosophy of Law series for helpful comments. I am also grateful to Ken Ehrenburg for his support and guidance in bringing this Element to fruition.

Cambridge Elements $\equiv$

Philosophy of Law

Series Editor
George Pavlakos
University of Glasgow

George Pavlakos is Professor of Law and Philosophy at the School of Law, University of Glasgow. He has held visiting posts at the universities of Kiel and Luzern, the European University Institute, the UCLA Law School, the Cornell Law School and the Beihang Law School in Beijing. He is the author of *Our Knowledge of the Law* (2007) and more recently has co-edited *Agency, Negligence and Responsibility* (2021) and *Reasons and Intentions in Law and Practical Agency* (2015).

Gerald J. Postema
University of North Carolina at Chapel Hill

Gerald J. Postema is Professor Emeritus of Philosophy at the University of North Carolina at Chapel Hill. Among his publications count *Utility, Publicity, and Law: Bentham's Moral and Legal Philosophy* (2019); *On the Law of Nature, Reason, and the Common Law: Selected Jurisprudential Writings of Sir Matthew Hale* (2017); *Legal Philosophy in the Twentieth Century: The Common Law World* (2011), *Bentham and the Common Law Tradition*, 2nd edition (2019).

Kenneth M. Ehrenberg
University of Surrey

Kenneth M. Ehrenberg is Professor of Jurisprudence and Philosophy at the University of Surrey School of Law and Co-Director of the Surrey Centre for Law and Philosophy. He is the author of *The Functions of Law* (2016) and numerous articles on the nature of law, jurisprudential methodology, the relation of law to morality, practical authority, and the epistemology of evidence law.

Associate Editor
Sally Zhu
University of Sheffield

Sally Zhu is a Lecturer in Property Law at University of Sheffield. Her research is on property and private law aspects of platform and digital economies.

About the Series

This series provides an accessible overview of the philosophy of law, drawing on its varied intellectual traditions in order to showcase the interdisciplinary dimensions of jurisprudential enquiry, review the state of the art in the field, and suggest fresh research agendas for the future. Focussing on issues rather than traditions or authors, each contribution seeks to deepen our understanding of the foundations of the law, ultimately with a view to offering practical insights into some of the major challenges of our age.

Cambridge Elements ☰

Philosophy of Law

Printed in the United States
by Baker & Taylor Publisher Services